Dancing
with Dogs

Dancing with Dogs

Easy-to-learn techniques and fun
routines for you and your dog

Mary Ray

& Andrea McHugh

THUNDER BAY
P·R·E·S·S

San Diego, California

Thunder Bay Press
An imprint of the Advantage Publishers Group
5880 Oberlin Drive, San Diego, CA 92121-4794
www.thunderbaybooks.com

All notations of errors or omissions should be
addressed to Thunder Bay Press, Editorial
Department, at the above address. All other
correspondence (author inquiries, permissions)
concerning the content of this book should be
addressed to Hamlyn, a division of Octopus
Publishing Group Ltd, 2–4 Heron Quays, London
E14 4JP, England.

ISBN-13: 978-1-59223-531-5
ISBN-10: 1-59223-531-X

Library of Congress Cataloging-in-Publication Data
available on request.

Printed and bound in China

1 2 3 4 5   10 09 08 07 06

No dogs were harmed in the making of this book.

Unless the information given in this book is
specifically for female dogs, dogs are referred to
throughout as "he." The information is equally
applicable to both male and female dogs, unless
otherwise specified.

Contents

Foreword

Is it just me, or do you sometimes get the feeling that life is too tough and there is no more fun to be had? We have stress on the job, family problems, endless unsatisfying chores, rising costs on all fronts, and no relief in sight. Then when you read the newspaper, watch TV, or turn on the radio, and you see a photo, view a video, or hear people talking about dancing with their dogs, it will bring a smile to your face, distract you from your problems, and make you reach down, hug your dog, and want what those people in the news have—a little fantasy and a little fun. Welcome to an activity that has captured imaginations worldwide: dancing with dogs!

But why are you just sitting there reading, watching, or listening? You do have your dog there, right? So get out and get dancing with your dog! Do it in the backyard, the park, or on the front porch—even in the closet—just do it! Plan a costume, choose the dog collar, dream up the dramatic moves, and get lost in a world that is fun and stress-free.

Trust me, there is no greater stress relief for a pet owner than dancing with your dog. Dogs are social animals and love to have verbal and physical interaction with their owners; nothing gives more pleasure to you and your dog than to dance to the music! Sharing and bonding are what life is all about, and sharing and bonding with our pets can bring so much satisfaction and peace to each of us. Canine freestyle, or dancing with dogs, is all about having fun and gaining an inner peace in your life with your dog, a peace that channels into all other aspects of your existence. Canine freestyle is also a way to incorporate some of the things you love most—your pet, music, dancing, creativity, and exercise—into one fun activity.

This wonderful book by Mary Ray offers activities to suit any fancy. There is something here for everyone—pet owner to expert canine freestyler—including beginner moves like spins and those tough advanced moves using props. Have fun, and when the going gets tough, get your dog and dance! And if you really love it, we will see you competing very soon!

Patie Ventre
Founder and President
World Canine Freestyle Organization

Introduction

In 1990, the first heelwork to music (HTM) routine came about almost accidentally, when John Gilbert, the well-known British agility competitor, asked Mary Ray to produce a training seminar, which he then set to music. When she performed the routine with her dog Toddy, he moved so well to the music that the routine appeared choreographed! People went away saying they had seen Mary doing a heelwork to music routine, and things began to evolve from there. A year later, Mary had begun to choreograph the routines and was invited to perform at Crufts, the world's largest dog show.

INTERNATIONAL INTEREST

It was not long before interest in heelwork to music began to take off in Canada and the United States. Sandra Davis, performing with her collie Pepper, began to introduce some very different, innovative moves that took the sport into a completely new dimension. International organizations were formed, and trainers began to produce videos and books that encouraged more people to give it a try.

COMPETITIVE DANCING

In 1991, the first HTM events started in Canada, and in 1993 the Musical Canine Sport International organization was formed there. The first HTM events in the United States were in 1992, and leading figures included Terry Arnold and Sandra Davis. In 1996, British trainer Peter Lewis organized the first HTM competition in the UK. The competition was such a success that it became an annual event. The rules were formalized, and the UK Kennel Club set up a working committee to move the sport to new levels.

DANCING FOR EVERYONE

Heelwork to music is not all about competing. One of the main advantages of the sport is how much it widens the scope of a dog's agility training. Even if you never intend to compete, the training in this book will teach your dog a completely new way of moving and make basic training easier and more interesting. For anyone who thinks dog training is boring, just try doing it to music. You will soon change your mind!

HEELWORK TO MUSIC TIMELINE

1990 Mary Ray performs her first unchoreographed HTM routine in the UK.

1991 The first seminar on HTM is held in Canada.

1991 Tina Martin and her golden retriever, Cognac, do an HTM demonstration at the Pacific Canine Showcase in Vancouver.

1991 The first freestyle competition held in Canada.

1992 Mary Ray's first choreographed routine is demonstrated at Crufts in the UK.

1992 First HTM events held in the United States.

1993 Formation of the Musical Canine Sport International in Canada. Rules for the sport are established.

1994 Formation of the Canine Freestyle Federation Inc. in the United States.

1996 First annual HTM competition held in the UK.

1998 Formation of the World Canine Freestyle Organization in the United States.

1998 First HTM competition held in Australia.

1999 Formation of the UK's first HTM club, Paws n Music.

2000 First HTM competition held in New Zealand.

2001 Formation of Canine Freestyle GB.

2002 Formation of the Musical Dog Sport Association in the United States.

2003 The Kennel Club of Great Britain officially recognizes and licences HTM as a sport.

2004 Mary Ray is invited to South Korea to demonstrate HTM.

2005 Mary Ray gives an HTM demonstration at the World Agility Championships in Spain. The first HTM competition was held at Crufts.

The basics
Heelwork versus freestyle

You may be wondering what the difference is between a heelwork to music (HTM) routine and a freestyle routine. Below are some basic definitions, but the rules vary from country to country, and as the sport progresses they are constantly being developed.

HEELWORK TO MUSIC

During a heelwork to music routine, the dog works off the lead but must remain on the right- or left-hand side of the handler or in other close positions. At least half of the moves should be about basic heelwork, but some other moves can be included, such as sidestepping, leg weaving, twists, and circles. The handler is allowed to sit or lie down during the routine if that is necessary. In some countries, there are stipulations that specify the compulsory elements that must be seen in a competitor's performance.

FREESTYLE

In a freestyle routine, the dog works off the lead but the routine can contain movements in any position. Basic heelwork is still used to link the moves together. Freestyle gives many more creative opportunities and generally allows the use of more props to enhance a routine. Handlers can dress up in costumes if they want to, and the dogs can wear dressed collars. Some competitions also allow ankle bands.

DOG COSTUMES

When dressing up a dog, stick to a simple collar or neckwear so that the dignity of the dog is maintained. This is important if freestyle and heelwork to music are to develop as serious sports.

PROPS

If you are doing a demonstration, you can use whatever props you like to help your performance. However, in competition it is best to check with the organizers because the rules can vary from country to country. Props are generally allowed in a routine provided they are integral to the performance in some way. Food and toys are not allowed into the ring, and care should be taken that any props used cannot be perceived as some kind of training aid. Typical examples of props in the routines in this book include a soccer ball, an umbrella, a matador's cape, a wizard's cane, a basket, or a fake bunch of flowers. For further information on props, see page 70.

Hat

Umbrella

Matador's cape

Hoop

Cane

Soccer ball

COMPETITIVE PERFORMANCES

A heelwork to music performance is usually judged in three sections, each of which is worth a maximum of ten points. These sections are:

Performance content

This includes how well the program flows, the number of movements, and, importantly, that the movements of the dog have a greater impact than those of the handler. Remember, the dog should always be the star in heelwork to music!

Accuracy and execution of movements

This looks at the quality of the partnership between the dog and his handler, the accuracy of the moves, and how willing and happy the dog appears to be in his work. Persistent barking will be marked down. The bearing and deportment of the handler will also be scored.

Musical interpretation

The handler and dog are judged on their ability to interpret the music. Although a handler may be expressive, the emphasis is always on the dog's movements, and the entire routine should complement the music.

What you will need

Along with lots of patience and enthusiasm, there are a few essential items that you will need for training your dog to perform heelwork to music, including training aids, toys, treats, music equipment, and comfortable clothes.

CLICKERS

Clickers are small, lightweight training devices with a metal tongue or button that clicks when pushed down. The sound informs the dog when he is doing something correctly. A food reward is given after clicking, and the dog soon associates the click with his reward.

Button clicker

A button clicker has a push button that, if necessary, can be activated under your foot. When training, it can be useful to operate the clicker under your foot, leaving both hands free to hold a lure. A button clicker is quiet and especially useful when working on paw work close to the dog's head.

Box clicker

This training device has the tongue set inside the clicker, which is activated by your thumb. It is louder than the other clickers, and care must be taken near a dog's head, as the noise may bother him. A box clicker is less likely to go off accidentally, so it can be more accurate.

TARGET STICK

This is an extending metal stick to which you can attach a foam ball or other prop. The extra length that a target stick provides to a handler's arm is very useful. Many different types of moves can be developed and created as the dog learns to target the stick with either his nose or paws. See page 27 for more details.

PUPPY PEN

A puppy pen is usually made of lightweight, hinged-wire fencing that can be folded into a variety of shapes and flattened for easy storage afterward. It can be useful as a barrier to teach some moves that require distance between you and your dog, for instance, when teaching your dog to circle around you (see page 55).

Button clicker

Box clicker

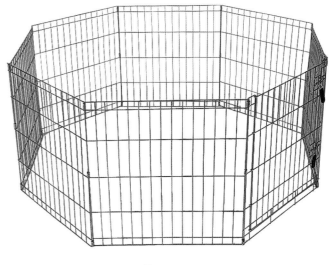

Puppy pen

TOYS

During training, toys can be useful both as a lure and as a reward. Some dogs prefer tug toys, which are readily available in pet stores and supermarkets. Others like to retrieve a ball or are motivated by noisy toys. Use a variety, and keep a couple of favorites for training sessions.

CD/cassette player

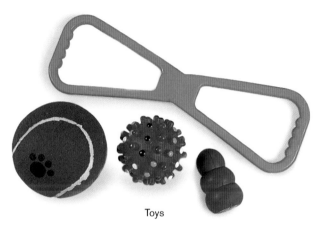

Toys

TREATS

Try a variety of treats to reward your dog, including chicken, mild hard cheese, sausages, or frankfurters, all of which can be cut into bite-size pieces and are easily visible when thrown. Dry dog treats can also be used but may become less effective than other treats. They are also difficult to break without crumbling and take longer to eat.

Keep treats close at hand, in a small container or a hip sack. Vary the treats you use, so your dog doesn't become bored and you can keep him interested longer.

CD OR CASSETTE PLAYER

A CD or cassette player is essential, along with a variety of music. Investing in good-quality speakers will help carry the sound. You may need a pair of earphones if practice sessions are in the early morning or later at night.

VIDEO RECORDER

A video recorder is useful for researching costumes and ideas and assessing your own routines.

COMFORTABLE CLOTHES

Tracksuits and a pair of good-quality, nonslip shoes or sneakers are ideal. Avoid long skirts or clothing that restricts your movement and could obstruct your dog. However, if your costume for a routine has a skirt or flapping material, make sure that you do a dress rehearsal so that your dog gets used to it before the big day.

TRAINING FACILITIES

It is best to do your training at home, either on a carpeted or nonslip floor, or in the yard. Some people rent a hall or train in a parking lot or at the beach, but remember, this will attract onlookers!

HAVE FUN!
One essential item for heelwork to music is your sense of humor. Keep it safe, and don't lose it— dancing with dogs is all about you and your dog having fun.

Treats

Finding a trainer

Your dog will need to undertake a basic level of obedience training before he starts to learn heelwork to music or freestyle. Beginners are advised to go to training classes, but it's very important to do some research and find the right professional trainer who is able to give you confidence and motivate you and your dog to enjoy the lessons. For some obedience training lessons to practice at home, see pages 20–23.

BASIC OBEDIENCE TRAINING

Take time to choose a dog club or trainer that uses positive, reward-based training. Avoid anyone who advocates the use of choke collars, which are old-fashioned and ineffective. Unfortunately, in some parts of the world these are still used, as are "training" collars that emit low-voltage electric shocks and "pinch" collars that dig into the dog's neck.

Personal recommendation is a good starting place when it comes to finding an obedience trainer. Your veterinarian may know of some local trainers, or you can ask friends and other dog handlers if they know of a class. You may find trainers advertising in the newspaper or phone book, but remember, anyone can rent a space, throw down some mats, and advertise as a dog trainer, and much harm can be done if the wrong kind of training is followed.

Assessing a trainer

All dogs (and their handlers!) are different, and some take longer to learn new skills than others. A trainer should acknowledge this within a group and be willing to spend time helping each and every dog understand the lessons. If you have an unusual or rare breed of dog, find out the trainer's views on the breed before you start classes.

If the response is very negative, then you are unlikely to enjoy that particular trainer's classes. Equally, some breeds are more agile than others, and the concentration span of all dogs will vary, so go and watch a few classes and see how the trainer deals with these anomalies. Watch what happens if there is a problem in the class, such as one dog becoming aggressive toward another, and see how the trainer responds. Physical punishment should be avoided at all times—training is supposed to be fun and a positive experience for you and your dog!

Things to consider

- Has the trainer been recommended to you?
- Have you attended some classes to observe the trainer in action?
- Does the trainer use positive, reward-based methods?
- Are choke chains discouraged?
- Do the dogs in the class look happy?
- Does the trainer motivate and inspire the other handlers?
- Do you feel confident about asking questions?
- Does the training area have a nonslip floor?
- Are there indoor and outdoor training facilities?

What your dog needs to know

Your dog should know the following before commencing heelwork to music training:

- 🐾 Basic obedience work ("sit," "stay," "wait," and "down").
- 🐾 Good general control (not pulling on the leash).
- 🐾 How to behave around other dogs.
- 🐾 Ability to walk to heel off the leash.
- 🐾 Ability to come back to you when called.

HTM TRAINING

If your local dog trainer or club doesn't have courses or know of a heelwork to music trainer in your area, contact your local or national kennel club or one of the many heelwork to music organizations (see Useful Contacts, page 125), who may be able to help. The Internet and libraries can also be great sources of information. No matter where you live, you should be able to find someone who can help you. Many organizations are happy to offer advice or arrange an introductory training day or workshop for interested individuals. If there is nothing available in your area but you know there are a few people interested, you could always consider starting your own group.

Learning at home

Read as much as you can about heelwork to music, and try to watch a few training videos. Doing your homework and getting as much information as you can on the sport, perhaps by watching some training classes or shows, will give you an idea of the standard required and the moves and routines that are being performed by other competitors.

Suitable breeds

In the early days of the sport, there were many dogs competing, from working to pastoral or gundog breeds. Collies, German shepherds, and retrievers find heelwork to music very easy, but any breed can perform, although some find it easier than others.

INFINITE VARIETY

Today, there is a huge variety of breeds competing, and at almost every show you will see a new competitor with a different type of dog, proving that all breeds are capable of performing at some level. Some of the shorter, stockier breeds, such as bulldogs, are harder to train due to their shape and physical limitations, but as long as a dog is fit, willing, and happy to work, there should not be a problem. It is advisable to get a dog checked out by a veterinarian to preclude any physical problems before you begin training.

Breed characteristics

Some people will argue that a particular breed of dog is difficult to train or can't do heelwork to music for some reason, perhaps because it has been bred for hunting.

Although it is true that some dogs have been bred for certain traits, the trick is for you to be more interesting than anything the dog has been bred for. There will always be dogs that are eager to work, while others have to be motivated with treats or toys. However, once a dog has learned something, you will find he enjoys doing it, so it's worth the effort.

TRAINER'S TIP

❧ Male dogs and bitches perform equally well in heelwork to music, and I have no preference to working with either but find that they need a different approach to training. Bitches tend to be softer and easier to handle, while dogs can be more dominant.

DANCING BREEDS

Here are just some of the breeds that have competed successfully in HTM classes:

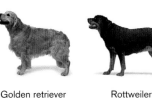

Poodle

Jack Russell

Great Basset Griffon Vendeen

Dalmatian

American cocker spaniel

Collie

Golden retriever

Rottweiler

Sheepdog

German shepherd

Great Dane

Bull terrier

Moves to suit you and your dog

When developing the choreography of a routine, or what moves you are going to ask your dog to do, you must apply some common sense. Take into account the dog's age, size, physical condition, confirmation, and personality.

YOUNG DOGS

You can start working with puppies when they are quite tiny. They are very responsive and supple, so it's easy to teach them some of the bending moves such as twisting and leg weaving. You should not teach puppies how to stand up on their back legs or jump over an object until they are at least a year old, because their bones will not be sufficiently developed. With some of the heavier breeds, it is advisable to wait even longer.

OLDER DOGS

It can be more challenging to work with older dogs, simply because they are less supple and may find some of the moves more difficult to do. The important thing to remember is to adjust your routines to accommodate your dog's constantly changing physical abilities. An older dog may no longer be able to do prolonged work on his back legs that he was happy to do previously.

DOG SIZE

Smaller dogs can be good for using props such as baskets or jumping into your arms. You will have to adapt jumping moves so that they can manage them easily, especially if you are using two dogs of different sizes in a routine. A small dog can be trained to jump over or run under a large dog. This really highlights the difference in their sizes, and audiences love it.

Working with a small dog

Small dogs who may find it difficult to keep close to your knee will find it easier to target a patch on your trousers. Be careful with your footwork when working with a small dog, because if you step on them they will lose confidence.

YOUR DOG'S PERSONALITY

Think about your dog's personality and the way that he moves. Is he a flamboyant, bubbly type or more reserved and serious? Would he be best suited to classical, jazz, or pop music? This will help you when considering which moves to select to show off his personality and abilities. Bear in mind that heelwork to music brings even the most reserved dogs out of themselves as they begin to thrive on the applause and attention.

MOVES TO SUIT YOU

You will need to consider your own physical abilities when developing routines, but most moves can be easily adapted. People of all ages and those with disabilities can still participate in the sport—walking sticks and crutches can make great targets or props!

Obedience training
Motivating your dog

The key to keeping a dog motivated is to make training as fun and interesting as you possibly can for him. Reward him generously with high-value toys or treats, and give him lots of praise when he does something well.

NO PUSHOVER

It is best not to train dogs by pushing or pulling them into position. You need to encourage dogs to follow a lure and figure out for themselves how they need to move. When you push a dog, he will automatically push back, so it is better to train him to do something such as sitting without putting a hand on him. The dog will also learn more quickly this way.

ONE TRICK AT A TIME?

You can teach more than one move during a training session. Variety is the spice of life and helps maintain motivation. Dogs only get confused if the moves are too similar or signals and commands are unclear. If this happens, go back a stage, then break the move down into smaller stages and reward frequently.

STAY CALM

Training sessions should always be reward-based, and no punishment should be used. Frequently reward and praise behaviors you want, and ignore those that you don't want. With this approach, your dog will enjoy training and remain motivated in the hope of getting another reward. If you find yourself losing patience, go back to something the dog knows and understands. End the session on a good note before you lose your temper.

WHEN TO REWARD?

When it comes to dogs, being mean won't keep them keen! People are often too mean with treats and expect a dog to do a lot of work in exchange for a tiny piece of food. The more rewards a dog gets when you are teaching him something new, the quicker he will learn it, so break each move down into tiny steps and reward constantly.

TIME FACTOR

If you only train a dog to work for a few minutes, that is all the time he will ever want to give you. To compete, however, you must increase the time the dog trains so that he develops the mental and physical stamina to complete a routine. Most routines are two to six minutes, but when your dog is competing, he will be faced with many distractions and will need to be able to concentrate for much longer.

MAINTAINING MOTIVATION

If your dog is losing motivation or shutting down mentally, stop what you are doing. Change the treat or toy, and do something you know he enjoys. Whatever happens, ensure that the session is a positive experience and always end on a positive note so that the dog doesn't lose confidence. However, don't get into the habit of allowing the dog to dictate when a session should end!

THE GOLDEN RULES OF TRAINING

- ❖ Collect high-value toys and treats, and keep them only for use in training sessions.
- ❖ Resist the temptation to push or pull your dog into the correct position.
- ❖ Gradually increase the length of training sessions to develop your dog's stamina.
- ❖ Keep sessions fun, and end on a positive note, doing something the dog enjoys.
- ❖ Reward immediately and frequently.
- ❖ Use your voice enthusiastically to praise.
- ❖ If your dog becomes confused, revert to an earlier stage and break the move down into smaller parts.

TRAINER'S TIP

❖ If your dog suddenly loses interest in his work or has problems with a move, ask a veterinarian to rule out a physical cause. It is easy for a dog to injure himself while he is out on a walk or when he is training, and there is often no obvious sign for you to see, so a professional opinion is essential.

On command

One of the keys to successful training is to use clear signals and commands. Whether you are using a clicker device or a verbal command, timing is crucial. Good timing will ensure that your dog understands exactly what behavior you want him to repeat.

CLICKER TRAINING

As soon as your dog performs a move correctly, use the clicker immediately, and then reward. If you click a second too early or late, you are not marking the behavior you want. Incorrect timing is the main cause of failed clicker training.

Gradually, the reward becomes less necessary and is replaced by a verbal command or signal. Phase out rewards slowly, introducing a random element to them. This encourages motivation, because the dog will be eager to perform and earn the reward.

Clicker timing

Think of the clicker as a type of camera that you use to "capture" the split second your dog performs a particular move. Timing is crucial. When using a camera, if you click too soon you won't record the picture you wanted. When using a clicker, if you press too early or late, you capture a different behavior than the one you wanted, and your dog will not know what to repeat. The clicker can "capture" subtle movements such as the shake of a head, but try not to accidentally click unwanted behaviors like barking.

Clicker training encourages the dog to figure out for himself what you want. This helps to build confidence, and the behavior becomes entrenched more quickly.

How to use the clicker

Clickers can be used in either hand or under your foot. The method is always the same:

1 Lure your dog to perform the behavior you want.
2 Immediately click and throw or give a treat.
3 Continue these two stages until the lure becomes a signal to the dog.
4 Add a verbal command to the behavior.
5 Repeat several times until the dog understands and repeats the move on command.
6 Eventually, the dog should be able to perform the move simply from your verbal command or signal.

VERBAL COMMANDS

You are allowed to use verbal commands and words of encouragement during a heelwork to music competition, so don't be afraid to do so. However, to keep the performance polished, try to be discreet so that the audience is unaware.

When giving a verbal command to your dog, speak clearly and authoritatively. Ask for upward moves in a higher voice than lower moves. For example, "down" is said in a lower tone than "over." Avoid similar-sounding commands, and reduce the risk of confusion by using the same commands with every dog that you work with. Remember to praise your dog enthusiastically.

HAND SIGNALS

Use the hand on the side closest to your dog to lure or give hand signals. When teaching your dog, exaggerate hand signals by making them larger than normal. As your dog learns, hand movements can become surprisingly subtle.

USING REWARDS EFFECTIVELY

Food rewards should be easily visible and not crumble when thrown—the last thing you want is your dog searching for scraps. The treat should take no longer than three seconds for the dog to eat and swallow. If he takes longer, choose something he is more interested in or can chew and swallow faster.

When starting a training session, take a handful of treats from your container or hip sack and throw a couple out so that the dog knows you have them. Throwing treats is an effective way of rewarding moves done at a distance and helps prevent the dog from associating your hand with food.

How to lure

Food can be used to lure a dog so that he follows your hand. This is most effective when combined with clicker training. Hold food firmly in an overhand or underhand position, but ensure that it is visible and can be smelled or licked but not snatched.

Where you hold the treat in relation to your dog will influence your dog's entire body movement. Holding it high over his nose will bring his head up and send his tail down to the floor, making the "sit" command much easier. It's a good idea to experiment with this before starting to ask for heelwork to music moves.

SOME USEFUL VERBAL COMMANDS

"Down"	Dog lies down	page 22
"Wait"	Dog stays still	page 23
"In front"	Dog stands in front, facing you	page 24
"Close"	At heel (dog's head at your left knee)	page 25
"Touch and tap"	Dog touches your hand or prop with paw	page 32
"Face"	Dog puts paw to face	page 36
"OK"	Dog knows that a command is finished	page 37
"Watch"	Dog looks at you	page 38
"Both"	Dog puts both paws up, either at a sit or stand	page 40
"Back"	Dog walks backward	page 41
"Through"	Dog goes through your legs from the front	page 42
"Between"	Dog goes through your legs from behind	page 42
"Around"	Dog circles around you	page 54

TRAINER'S TIP

🐾 Barking is discouraged in performances, and if your dog barks a lot during training, he is probably confused or frustrated. Stop what you are doing and go back to what he last understood, then try giving clearer commands and signals.

Gaining control

Basic obedience training is best achieved by going to classes (see page 12), but here are some valuable lessons for you to practice at home with your dog. Always remember that teaching should be based on the positive reinforcement of good behavior.

TAKE THE LEAD

Your dog will need to be able to work off the leash to do his routines. Before starting work off the leash, make sure he can walk calmly in a straight line without pulling you. Use a long leash with an ordinary collar. Check the fit of the collar by ensuring that you can easily slide a couple of fingers underneath it. Never use choke collars, which attempt to work by punishing negative behavior. Teaching should be aimed at positively reinforcing good behavior.

Introduce clicker training early to encourage your dog to keep close to your leg and look up at you in anticipation of a reward. Clicker training is a very effective way of affirming this behavior. Don't forget to offer verbal praise as well!

Circle work

Your dog will soon begin to understand where you want him to be, and when this happens you can begin working him in a large circle. Keep the dog on a leash, but position yourself on the inside of the circle with the dog on the outside of the circle to promote a free flow of movements. To encourage this free movement, hold the leash out in front of you and walk forward on the circle for a few paces. If the dog remains calmly focused on you and doesn't pull on the leash, click and offer a reward.

Once your dog has mastered this, you should begin to build in the verbal command "close" or "heel" for the position and then start working on changes of pace and direction.

TRAINER'S TIP

🐾 If your dog starts to pull while on the leash, simply stand still and wait until he stops or turns toward you. The second the leash goes slack, click. Now walk toward the dog so that he is in the heelwork position on your left side. Only offer him a treat when you are side by side, with the dog on a loose leash. The more you practice, the quicker he will learn that not pulling earns him a reward.

Walking on a leash

Nervous dogs often seem more confident walking on a relaxed, loose leash. Being restrained on a short, tight leash can increase their anxiety, as they may anticipate a dangerous situation. Dominant dogs are likely to be less confident on a loose leash, as they prefer to be "top dog" and lead you around.

RECALL

Getting your dog to come back whenever you call him is one of the most important lessons he must learn. The sooner you start to teach this, the easier it will be. There is nothing more frustrating for an owner than to be left repeatedly shouting a dog's name while the dog ignores him and continues to romp away with his friends.

The key to instant recall in the face of any distraction is to ensure that you, the handler, are more worthwhile and interesting than anything else the dog may have seen.

Begin by practicing in an enclosed, secure room where there are very few distractions. Take the dog off the leash and allow him to wander around freely as you walk a few steps away. Now call his name and rattle your treat container to get his attention. The second he looks at you, click. When he returns, immediately offer him a reward.

Recall dos and don'ts

🐾 Don't lose your temper and punish your dog if he doesn't return to you immediately. This simply confirms to him that returning to you is a negative experience and will make it more difficult for you to get him back next time.

🐾 Don't make the recall command into a game. Some dogs think it is great fun to get you to chase them, and if you indulge them, you will affirm that this is an effective way of getting your attention.

🐾 If you are going into a situation where there will be many distractions and you might have trouble getting your dog to come back to you, change your treats to those that are of higher value to him.

The four commandments

Teaching "sit," "stand," "down," and "wait" properly will reap dividends in the future. Remember to vary the tone of your voice when giving verbal commands. Use a higher tone for "stand," a middle tone for "sit," and a lower tone for "down."

SIT

This can be done from a "stand" or "down" position. The key to achieving the "sit" is positioning the dog's nose correctly at the start. With his nose high, the hindquarters naturally lower and he is already halfway into a sit. With his head and nose low, his hindquarters will lift, making the move more difficult.

1 With a clicker in one hand, hold a treat in the other and call your dog to you. Hold your treat hand out so that the dog is positioned at arm's length directly in front.

2 Turn your treat hand to the overhand position and raise it directly above the dog's nose. Don't hold it too high, or he may jump up. Push your hand out slightly toward the dog's tail. This naturally encourages the dog's nose up, tips his head back, and lowers his hindquarters. As soon as he drops into a sit, click and reward.

3 Repeat, gradually building in the verbal command "sit" as soon as the dog's hindquarters drop.

DOWN

When teaching the "down" position, you should put the dog into a sit to start.

1 Hold the clicker in one hand and a treat in the other in an underhand position just below the dog's nose. This will lower his nose and head down, making the down move easier.

2 Now lure the treat diagonally forward and downward. You want him to move only his front legs toward you, so progress slowly. When he cannot reach any farther forward with his front legs, move the treat to the floor.

3 As he sinks down, click and reward. Repeat several times, introducing the "down" command.

STAND

Teach the "stand" command to get your dog up again. This move should be smart and snappy, and can be taught from either the "sit" or "down" position. The dog should push up from behind rather than hauling himself up, with minimum effort on his front legs.

From "sit"

1 With your dog in the "sit" position, hold the clicker in one hand and a treat in the other, close to his nose. Take a step backward, pulling the treat hand slightly toward you.

2 Keep the treat level with your dog's nose, and when he stands, click and reward. Gradually build in the verbal command "stand." Alternatively, you can slide a favorite toy or his food bowl toward him, positioning it between his front legs, directly under his chin. He will have to lift his hind legs to reach the toy or bowl.

From "down"

1 Put your dog in the "down" position with the clicker in one hand and a treat in the other, close to his nose.

2 Take one step backward, simultaneously moving your hand up and across to raise his nose and his legs. When he stands, click and reward. Gradually build in the verbal command "stand."

TRAINER'S TIP

🐾 An upright "down" position, where the dog drops down with his four legs under him, is useful for when you need him to move again, such as for a creeping weave. Luring the dog into a flat "down," where he is lying on his side, is useful for teaching moves like the rollover.

WAIT

Teaching your dog to wait patiently is very useful, especially when he starts anticipating movements. You can combine the "wait" command with other moves such as "stand, wait" or "sit, wait."

1 Put your dog in a "stand" or "sit" position, but make him wait for a couple of seconds, then click and reward. Slowly increase the wait time before clicking and rewarding to about six seconds. Introduce the command "wait."

2 Once he has learned this, give the "stand, wait" or "sit, wait" command and walk away. The dog must wait for a few seconds before you return and reward. Slowly increase the distance by one step, clicking at the further distance away, then returning and giving the reward.

Basic positions

Once a dog is working confidently off the leash, you can introduce him to some basic heelwork positions. These include "in front" and the "close" heelwork position on both sides, plus the ability to maintain his position tight to your leg while moving.

IN FRONT

This position forms the basis of many heelwork to music moves. It is incredibly useful, particularly if any confusion develops while you are doing a routine. Instead of panicking, you can simply ask for "in front" and start again.

1 Have a clicker in one hand and a treat in the other. Position your hands as if they are clasped together in front of you at waist level, with your elbows out at right angles. Your dog will soon associate this as the visual signal for "in front." Click when the dog is standing a couple of steps away.

2 Instead of just giving him the treat, throw it out to the side, about 6 feet away. Your dog will run and get his treat and then return to see if you are going to provide any more. Click when he is facing you and standing straight. Gradually introduce the command "in front" prior to clicking and treating.

3 Practice linking the "in front" position to other moves, such as "in front, sit" or "in front, down."

TRAINER'S TIP
🐾 Try to get the dog returning to you quickly and standing straight. To encourage this, withhold the click until the dog learns that it is how he returns and stands that earns him the reward.

CLOSE

"Close" is another important heelwork position and one that you will use all the time when training. Your dog must stay tight to your leg, which the "close" command teaches. Looping him in an arc behind teaches him to move his back end separately from the front.

1 Stand the dog in front, slightly off center, to your left. Keep your feet together and hold a treat in the overhand position, level with his nose.

2 Place your left foot one step back and use the treat to lure the dog behind, on your left, and then lure him back in a counterclockwise arc. Keep your hand close to the dog's nose when luring, and always turn him toward you, so his eyes stay focused on you.

3 Keep your left foot back and click when the dog steps around your leg and brings his hind legs into a position level with his head.

4 Close your feet together and give the treat when the dog is standing right beside you, with his nose close to your left knee.

5 Repeat on both sides, building in the command "close" prior to clicking.

When your dog understands the "close" command, you can stop luring and hold the treat close to your knee, at the point where you want his nose to be. As you say the word "close," your dog should react by immediately swinging his back end around and getting into position.

CLOSE WHILE MOVING

Your dog must maintain the heelwork position wherever you are. Ask him to get in close while you walk a large circle, keeping the dog on the outside.

1 Hold your treat hand at your side so that the dog has to look up—but not so high that it's uncomfortable for him or he swings his back end out. Settle for a few steps at first, clicking when he is in the correct position and moving well. Stop each time you reward, since he cannot take and eat his treat in the correct heelwork position.

2 Change direction so that the dog is on the inside. It is more difficult for him this way, so enlarge the circle. When he can do this well, he is becoming hindquarter aware, which is a good sign.

TRAINER'S TIP
🐾 Walk briskly—if you move too slowly, the dog will pace rather than trot. See page 28 for more details.

Target practice

The targeting technique, where your dog follows your hand or another object, opens up a whole new world of possibilities. You can encourage the popular high-stepping trot that audiences love or teach your dog to follow a prop such as the matador's cape in Viva España! (see page 101) or the disappearing cane in World of Magic (see page 116).

CHOOSING A TARGET

A dog can target your hand, a stick, or a marker such as a carpet tile. The click-and-treat training method encourages the dog to figure out whether you want him to target with his nose, mouth, or paws. Small dogs may find the conventional heelwork position at your knee difficult, so teaching them to target a point lower down, or a target stick, will help. Using a target stick with a small dog can also prevent backache.

TARGETING THE HAND

Start by teaching your dog to place his nose on or close to your hand. This will give you an easy way to guide him through moves without the use of lures.

1 Hold a clicker in one hand and have plenty of treats available. Hold a treat between the second and third fingers of your target hand so that it's easily seen and sniffed but can't be snatched.

2 Encourage the dog to sniff the treat, clicking when his nose touches it and then moving your target hand up out of his reach. Give the dog a treat from your other hand before re-presenting the target hand and repeating the sniff, touch, click, and treat.

3 Gradually ask him to move further out before touching your hand. Throw treats 3–6 feet away from you so that he has to move faster, and then put out your hand without holding a treat. Your dog should still sniff and touch, so be ready to click immediately and treat from your other hand. Introduce a verbal command such as "nose" or "pat," and begin to change the point of the click so that the dog understands he is clicked for following the target.

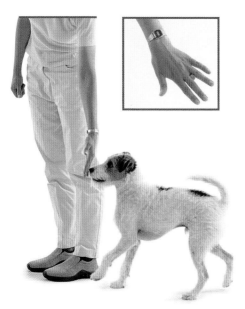

USING A TARGET STICK

A target stick is useful to get extra movement on circles or to step higher. Make the stick more interesting and visible by sticking a foam ball on the end.

1 Hold the stick out for your dog to sniff, and as soon as his nose touches, click and throw a treat out. This encourages him to move away and return to the stick. Introduce the command "nose" just before clicking.

2 Here's the fun part! Hold the stick out and encourage the dog to follow it. Change the click to when the dog is following rather than touching. Take him around in circles or a figure eight, or raise the stick higher to get him to stand up on his back legs. Moving it down between his front legs will encourage him to take a bow.

Give a paw

Put a piece of plastic or wood on the end of the target stick to support your dog's paw. Hold this out toward him, saying "give paw." The second the dog puts a paw onto the stick, click and give a treat. Like people, most dogs naturally favor their right or left side. Your dog will favor his dominant paw to touch, but you should encourage him to use both paws to make him more agile and balanced.

NOSE TARGETING

Teach your dog to target a specific object such as a plastic lid on the floor and touch it with his nose.

1 Put your dog in a "wait" position and place a treat on the lid. Return and tell him to get the treat. Click as soon as his nose touches the lid.

2 Repeat several times, introducing the command "nose." Stop putting a treat down, but as soon as the dog's nose touches, click and throw a treat away from it.

PAW TARGETING

For this you will need a larger target like a carpet tile.

1 Put your dog in the "wait" position and place a treat on the far side of the carpet tile. Return and tell him to get the treat. Click as soon as his front feet step on the carpet.

2 Repeat several times, introducing the command "on your mark." Stop putting a treat down, but continue to click and treat when his front feet step onto the target.

How your dog moves

Dogs have five paces of movement: walk, pace, trot, canter, and gallop. It is the trot pace—when your dog's legs are moving in diagonal pairs together—that is mostly used in heelwork to music dance routines.

PACING

Pacing, which is how dogs tend to move naturally, is less stylish than the trot pace. Pacing is an energy-saving pace, and if done in a routine, the audience will think the dog is not making any effort. The next time you are walking down the road with your dog, look down and you will usually see that he is pacing beside you—moving two legs on one side of his body and two on the opposite side. This is because, unless you are power walking, the dog will not be moving fast enough to maintain a trot.

HEALTH CHECK

If your dog insists on pacing all the time, don't assume that he's being lazy and not making enough of an effort. There may be an underlying physical problem that makes trotting difficult for him. Always get a veterinarian to check the dog if you are concerned about any aspect of his movement, health, or behavior.

STEPPING UP A GEAR

When working a dog in the heelwork position, with his head tilted upward and the focus higher, his legs will naturally lift up better in the trot. The trot also gives a much better, more natural level of impulsion, and as you may have observed, the higher the trot the more spectacular it looks.

Improving the pace

Some dogs are born with naturally fabulous paces, and others need help to develop their paces. If you work your dog actively on the outside of a circle (see page 25), he will usually change his pace from pacing to trotting. Exercising him in this way, changing pace and direction often, will help make him more balanced, agile, and enthusiastic about his work.

Gaits within routines

It's easy to develop an entirely new look to a routine simply by changing the way your dog moves or the level of the paces used within it. At a normal pace, the dog should be trotting, but by teaching him to target your hand (see page 26) or follow a prop (see page 27), you can extend or slow

the trot down, making it look more flamboyant and stylish. If a dog always trots at the same pace throughout a routine, it will not look as varied or interesting for the audience.

Supple up

Always work your dog on the left and right, because like most creatures, he will have a favored side and may move much more easily on this side than the other. You will probably find that, on the easier side, your dog will have few problems crossing his hind legs over. On the less favored side, however, the dog will tend to step one foot up to the other one, then stop short of actually crossing it. This is the reason why it is so important to work dogs in the heel position on the right leg as well as the left. Because this is often neglected, many dogs find crossing their hind legs to the left much more difficult. By practicing all of the moves equally on both sides, the dog will gradually build up the necessary muscle tone and achieve the required level of suppleness to perform at his best.

TRAINER'S TIPS

❧ Always start and finish your practice sessions by working your dog on his easiest side, and then gradually build up the length of time spent on the more difficult side until you are eventually working both sides equally.

❧ The basic position exercises on pages 24 and 25 will help your dog to develop back end awareness and that all-important crossover with his hind legs. The dog will find crossing his legs much easier if he is not standing too close in to you.

❧ Make your practice sessions more fun by putting on some upbeat music. This will help you to maintain rhythm, and you will also start to develop a feel for what kind of music suits your dog's personality and the way he moves.

Leave and retrieve

It's important that your dog can retrieve an object, return it to you, and release it immediately. The last thing you want in the middle of your routine is for the dog to run off with one of the props with you in hot pursuit! Teaching him to retrieve on command is vital, but it's easier to teach at this stage, after he's been taught to target an object with his nose.

LEAVE

Hopefully you will have been playing games with your dog since he was a puppy, and he will already be familiar with the command "leave." If you need to teach or reinforce this, however, try the following technique.

1 Use a tug toy so that you can easily keep a hold on it at all times. Encourage the dog to play with it, and when you want him to let go, say "leave." Don't engage in any more play; simply hang onto the toy and keep quiet until he lets go of his own accord.

2 The second he releases the toy, click and give him a treat. He will soon realize that the sooner he lets go, the quicker the play session can continue and the more treats he will get.

PERFORMANCE NOTES

🐾 Bear in mind how easy a prop will be for a dog to retrieve in a routine. For example, in the World of Magic routine (see page 116), the dog retrieves a fake bunch of flowers from your sleeve. To make the stems easier for him to get hold of, try wrapping tape around them.

RETRIEVE (FETCH)

Some dogs are not eager to pick up objects in their mouths. However, clicker training is probably the easiest way to teach a dog that is not a natural retriever to retrieve, or "fetch," an item.

1 Choose carefully the item you want the dog to retrieve—it should not be too large, heavy, or uncomfortable for him to want to hold in his mouth. Hold the item out to show him, and as he sniffs it, click and treat.

2 Do this a few times and then withhold the click. The dog will continue to sniff, but when he doesn't hear a click he will probably use his mouth to take the toy or prop. If your dog seems reluctant to hold the toy, change it for something softer or more interesting to him.

3 Each time the dog takes the item in his mouth, extend the time by a few seconds before you click and treat. When the dog actually holds the item in his mouth for a couple of seconds, click and treat.

4 Next, place the item on the floor. Wait until the dog goes to pick it up, then click and treat. Gradually place the toy further away from you, then wait until the dog comes back to you with it before you click and treat. You may have to click for just a step or two initially, but gradually withhold the click until he returns the toy.

5 The aim is to get the dog to pick up the toy and bring it back to you in one move. Now is the time to build in the retrieve command, which is "fetch." Don't do this before he understands what you are after, or he may associate the click and reward with chewing or dropping the toy rather than picking it up on command and returning it to you when you ask for it.

6 The final part of this important lesson is teaching the dog to keep holding the toy in his mouth until you decide to take it from him. Do this by withholding the click when he drops the toy, waiting until he picks it up again and giving the command "leave" as you take it from him. Click and treat as the dog releases the toy.

Practice with a variety of props that you may use in your routines. Suggested items are a small basket with a handle, a lightweight child's umbrella, or a fake bunch of flowers.

TRAINER'S TIP

❧ A dog may be reluctant to pick up an object because of its taste, weight, or texture, but if the toy you are offering is his favorite and he is reluctant to let it go, increase the value of the treats you are offering. By making what you are offering more exciting, he should soon be happy to retrieve and leave anything you ask him to.

Paw show
Basic paw moves

Simple paw moves include the "touch," "tap," shaking hands, and waving. Crowds love these moves, as they demonstrate a real bond between dog and handler. Later in this chapter, we look at other paw moves, such as covering the eyes and high fives.

TOUCH AND TAP

"Touch" and "tap" teach your dog to touch an object with his left or right paw, depending on your command.

1 Put the dog in a "sit" position and stand in front of him. Hold a clicker in one hand and a treat in the other, so the dog can sniff but not snatch the treat.

2 Put your treat hand close to the dog's nose but to the side so that he has to turn his head slightly. This will make him off balance and take the weight off the leg you want him to lift. Most dogs will try to open your hand with this paw to get the treat. Click when the dog touches your hand and offer the treat. If he seems reluctant, pick up his paw with your clicker hand, then click. The dog will soon associate lifting his paw with a reward.

3 Repeat on both sides, adding in the command "touch" for the left paw and "tap" for the right. Be consistent so that the dog won't confuse which paw to give.

SCRAPE AND DIG

The Viva España! routine (see page 101) involves the dog scraping the ground like a bull. You can teach your dog to scrape using the following method.

1 Hold a target mat out toward the dog and give the "touch" command so that the dog touches the mat with one of his paws. Click and treat in the normal way.

2 Keep repeating the command, saying "touch, touch, touch," so that the dog touches the mat repeatedly.

3 Now put the mat down on the floor and build in the "scrape" command. To encourage a digging movement with two paws, follow the above but say "touch, tap, touch, tap" repeatedly so that the dog touches the target mat with both paws. Gradually build in the command "dig."

PAWS AND PROPS

Once your dog understands the "touch" and "tap" commands, you can ask him to touch a prop such as an umbrella.

1 Put the dog into a "sit" position and hold out a closed umbrella or cane, giving the "touch" or "tap" command. Click as the dog reaches to put his paw on the prop, and give him a treat.

2 Add on the "wait" command to keep your dog's paw in place, and give the release command of "OK" to signal that the move is over.

Try some variations, such as the dog putting both paws around the umbrella or asking him to put both his paws on your outstretched hand. You could also try kneeling and holding one arm out or asking the dog to stand tall and placing both paws on your outstretched arm.

SHAKE ON IT

Teaching your dog to shake hands looks effective and is a useful way to signal the start or finish of a routine.

1 Develop the "touch" and "tap" commands into a handshake by kneeling down in front of your dog while holding a treat in one hand and opening the palm of your other hand, inviting him to place his paw there. Click when he touches your open palm and offer the treat. Repeat on both sides.

2 Kneel up and repeat, keeping the dog in "sit" and clicking as he lifts the correct paw.

3 Soon you should be able to stand, and your dog will lift a paw on the command "how do you do?" or "say hello." Your open hand will cue which paw you want.

WAVING

Concentrate on asking for the wave with one front paw (perhaps the dog's favored side). This will help prevent any confusion, such as swapping paws to try to reach your hand.

1 Start by saying "give paw" (see page 27), but as the dog lifts his paw to touch or tap, move your hand up out of his reach. The dog should raise his paw higher to make contact. Click for this extra effort.

2 Repeat several times, clicking the paw at different heights. Don't ask him to raise his paw so high that he goes off balance and puts his foot down. Gradually delay the clicks until the dog raises and lowers his paw. Wait until he repeats this movement and build in the command "wave."

TRAINER'S TIP
🐾 Make the "wave" command easier for your dog to understand by linking it to the other commands in the handshake sequence. Open your palm and say "touch, touch" or "tap, tap," depending on whether you want him to use his right or left paw, then add on the word "wave." Once the wave is developed, you can drop the other commands.

On the move

When you are performing with your dog, you will often need to use moves that link one part of a routine to another. The following moves, including marching together and sideways steps, are ideal for this.

MARCHING TOGETHER

Teaching your dog to march in time with you looks stunning and is relatively easy to achieve.

1 Once your dog knows how to lift a paw on command (see page 32), use the "touch" and "tap" commands so that he touches one of your feet rather than a hand. Begin by standing, but keep the dog in "sit," and then progress to him standing in front and then in the heelwork position.

2 Lift your left foot and open the palm of your left hand. Your dog should follow the signal to lift his left paw. Now put your foot down and lift the right one, opening your right palm. Start with one or two steps, and then gradually build the sequence into a short march.

3 Once your dog understands, you can drop the hand signals because he will associate your raised foot with the paw you want him to lift.

SIDEWAYS MOVES

In this move, you and your dog will move sideways together, and your crossover steps will mirror each other. With the dog in the heelwork position on your left, if you move to the left you will be moving into him and if you move to the right you will be moving away from him. Hand targeting and the "close" or "move" commands help to achieve this move.

1 Begin by standing the dog to the side of you but not as tight to your leg as he would be for the "close" position. This is particularly important when moving to the left, so that you don't tread on his paws.

2 If you are going to step sideways to the right, cross your left foot over the front of your right foot while using the "pat" hand target command to maintain the dog's distance from you (see page 26).

3 Move your foot across, and as the dog targets your hand, he should move his paw across. If he leaves his back end out, you can give the "close" command to bring him back in again.

4 In the beginning, just click for a single crossover step, then reward, but gradually increase the number of steps into a sequence. Practice in both directions. When moving away from the dog to the right, you can build in the command "move."

BACK TO FRONT

You can also teach your dog to lift his hind legs on command. This is not as difficult as it might sound, as dogs have quite ticklish feet and will usually lift them easily with a bit of encouragement.

1 Ask your dog to stand, and kneel down beside him, holding a treat out close to his nose.

2 Touch or tickle the toes of one of his hind paws to encourage him to lift his foot off the ground, then click and treat to reward him. Repeat this technique several times, lightening your touch each time, and clicking and treating as soon as he lifts his paw.

3 Once your dog understands exactly what you are asking him to do, build in a command such as "foot" prior to clicking. He will soon begin to associate this word with the movement of lifting his hind leg.

4 Still kneeling down, continue to practice the move, but this time only giving the verbal command. Once your dog can lift his hind leg on command, practice with you in the upright position. Choose a different command for each hind leg, such as "paw" for the left foot and "foot" for the right.

5 At this point, you can start to join in by lifting your leg backward as you give your dog the verbal command. Performed successfully, this can look very effective.

TRAINER'S TIPS

🐾 Think of ways to incorporate specific moves into your routines. This move could be built into the Match of the Day routine (see page 86), as you both appear to warm up for the big match!

Face moves

Several opening and finishing poses in heelwork to music routines involve face moves, such as the dog covering one eye in a salute, hiding both eyes with his paws, or putting a paw over one or both sides of his nose. These moves can look very effective and will captivate the audience before you even start your routine. The Stars and Stripes routine (see page 80) begins with you and your dog saluting each other.

WIPING THE FACE

Face moves originate from the dog's natural tendency to clean his face with a paw. The trick is to encourage the dog to exhibit this behavior by finding something that will make him want to wipe his face. Place a lightweight leash or one of those small sticky notes found in offices over the dog's nose. He will be aware that there is something on his nose and will want to brush it away. Don't use something too lightweight or anything that will irritate him or stick to his fur, since he needs to be able to get it off easily using his paw.

1 Put the dog in the "sit" position and gently place the loop of the handle of a leash or the sticky note over his nose. Tell the dog to wait, and slowly move away from him. Take out your treat and clicker, and then give the release command (such as "OK") to signal that the wait is over and he can remove what is on his nose. Be ready to click as soon as his paw comes up to brush the leash or sticky note away, then offer him the treat.

2 Rub a piece of food such as chicken or cheese around the dog's muzzle to encourage him to use his paws on his face. Dogs will naturally try to clean their face by rubbing their nose on the carpet or using a paw. If your dog uses a paw, be ready to click and treat so that he understands this is the behavior you want.

3 Keep practicing until the dog understands that it is the action of wiping his face that earns him the click and treat, then build in the verbal command "face." Continue to practice until the dog can wipe at his face solely from

your verbal command. At this stage, you can gradually extend the time your dog holds his paw in position by telling him to wait or by withholding the click and treat you offer him.

TRAINER'S TIP
❧ Some dogs find it easier to learn face moves from the "down" position, as their paws are closer to their nose, so it comes to them more naturally.

HIDING THE EYES

Once your dog can understand and perform the "face" command, you can develop the move so that he places both of his paws over his nose at the same time, effectively hiding both eyes.

1 Choose a particularly tasty food treat, such as a piece of chicken or cheese, and, with your dog in the "down" position, wipe it gently on either side of the dog's nose. The dog will naturally try to rub this off with his paw, so be ready with the clicker as soon as he raises either one of his paws to his face.

2 Use a different command for this move, such as "hide," and keep practicing until he understands that you want him to wipe both paws over his face.

3 Be patient, and start to withhold the click until your dog has both paws in position. Once he puts both paws over his eyes, tell him to "wait" and gradually extend the length of the hold before you click and reward.

TRAINER'S TIP

❧ Why not try linking the "face" and "hide" commands to other moves? For example, you could add them to "bow" (see page 50), "down" (see page 22), or "beg" (see page 38), all of which look very effective.

"Hide" and "beg"

"Face" and "bow"

"Face" and "down"

RELEASE COMMAND

It is a good idea to develop a command that will let the dog know when a particular task or session has ended. You need to let the dog know that he can stop focusing his attention on you, and if you simply walk away from him he will find this very confusing. Do this from the early stages of his training, and whenever you finish something, use a verbal command such as "OK" or "finished," and reinforce this by offering him a treat or a toy.

Advanced moves
Crowd pleasers

The following moves are particularly popular with audiences. They include the beg, with the dog sitting on his haunches and lifting up both front paws, and the high five.

THE BEG

Use a button clicker to teach the beg, since it is quieter around the dog's ears. If you don't have one, hold your box clicker further away or try putting adhesive putty or a plastic sticker on it to dampen the sound.

1 Put the dog in "sit" in front of you, at arm's length. Hold a treat toward his nose, moving the hand up and back so that his head tilts back. This will encourage him to lift his front paws. As soon as both paws are off the ground, click and reward. He will probably put his feet right down again, until he becomes more balanced.

2 Some larger breeds will need support while performing this move. Put a hand under one paw and help lift it, taking the treat up over the dog's head to encourage him to bring the other paw up. Gradually withdraw your hand, then click and reward when he can hold the position for a second or two.

3 Repeat, but each time ask your dog to lift his paws a little higher to help him find his point of balance. Once the dog can hold the position for a few seconds, build in the command "beg."

LOOK AND WATCH

The "look" and "watch" commands teach your dog to focus his attention on you. When used in a routine, you will both appear to be looking at something in the distance and then at each other. Crowds love seeing this apparently secret communication between you both!

1 To teach your dog to "look," get him in the "close" position and hold his collar. Throw a toy or treat, and as the dog watches it land, say "look." Then click and give the release command—the reward is the food or toy you threw. Repeat this until you no longer have to hold the collar.

2 To teach the dog to watch you, every time your dog looks at you (use any opportunity for this), say the word "watch," then click and reward. Your dog will soon understand that he gets a treat for looking up at you.

GIVE ME FIVE!

Once the dog understands the handshake and beg, he should have little difficulty learning the high five. Just be careful not to position yourself too far away from him, or he may fall forward when trying to reach you.

1 Put the dog in "sit" and crouch down to his level. Give the "give paw" or "say hello" command for the handshake while holding out your open palm. As with the handshake, click and reward from the other hand as soon as he touches your hand.

2 Next, lift your hand up so that your palm is facing your dog and ask him to give you a paw. The moment he touches your hand, click and treat. When he does this successfully, build in the command "high five" as he goes to touch your hand.

3 Practice on the other side, using the "tap" and "touch" commands depending on which hand you are using. Once the dog can work just as easily from either side, he is ready to try the high five from the beg position.

4 Stand up and give the dog the "beg" command. Bend forward and hold out both hands with palms facing him, giving the "high five" command. Your dog should associate both hands with the command and touch both at the same time. Click and reward immediately.

TRAINER'S TIPS

🐾 A button clicker can be operated from under your foot when you are standing, leaving both hands free.

🐾 If your dog only makes contact with one paw, stand closer and put out the hand on his weaker side first.

🐾 Teach your dog to stand tall (see page 40) before you teach the high five from an upright position.

Upright moves

Don't ask for any upright work until your dog is at least twelve months old (it is advisable to wait slightly longer with some of the larger breeds). Small, lightweight dogs often find standing up on their hind legs second nature, but large heavyweights may struggle.

STANDING TALL

For all upright moves, you first need to teach the dog to stand up on his hind legs and hold his balance. Consider your dog's breed, size, age, and health before you try any upright moves, and continually assess his capabilities over time. It would be unfair to ask even the most talented of senior dogs to attempt the moves he did so easily in his youth, because it would put too much pressure on his joints.

1 With the dog standing in front, hold a treat in the overhand position so that he tilts his head up. Ask him to give a paw, and then as soon as he lifts it, move the treat up and slightly behind him. This will encourage him to push up onto his hind legs. Click and treat as soon as he lifts both front paws off the ground, before he has the chance to move his back legs. Repeat until the dog understands that you want him to lift both front legs off the ground.

2 Be patient and gradually increase the height that you ask your dog to lift his paws, as this will help him to improve his balance. Build in a verbal command such as "both," and eventually extend the time you click and reward until the dog can hold his balance for a couple of seconds.

TRAINER'S TIPS

🐾 Dogs tend to associate the word "both" with raising both their front paws off the ground and are not confused if they are asked for it in either the beg or the upright position.

🐾 Small dogs can be a little intimidated by a handler standing over them. If this is the case, practice this move in a kneeling position until your dog seems more confident.

WALKING TALL

Once a dog has learned to stand tall, he shouldn't have difficulty learning to take a few steps backward, forward, or sideways on command. Most dogs will do a kind of bunny hop when asked to walk forward, so it is easiest to teach them to walk backward first. Use a particularly high-value treat for this.

1 Stand about 6 feet away from the dog and hold the toy or treat out at arm's length in front of you. Give the "both" command for him to stand upright. Start to walk toward the dog, still holding the toy up and out in front. Your dog will have to take a step backward to continue focusing on the toy. When he takes a step back, click and treat. Set yourself and the dog up again so that you can retry.

2 When the dog finds his point of balance, wait until he takes a second step before you click and reward. Take your time and build the number of steps up very gradually. At this stage, you can build in the "back" command just before you click. Your dog will need to build up strength in his back legs, as well as his agility and confidence, to take more than a couple of steps.

UPRIGHT HIGH FIVE

Your dog will already know how to do the high five from the "sit" position, and now he is ready to try this from the upright position. If he seems confused, go back to asking for the high five in the "sit" and then try again.

1 Stand in front of the dog and give the "both" command to get him in the upright position. Now you can give the "high five" command, holding out your hands, palms facing toward the dog.

2 As your dog reaches up to touch one or both of your hands, click and reward. Practice until your dog can make contact with both of your hands at the same time.

TRAINER'S TIP

Don't support a dog as he walks on his hind legs, because you can't assess if he's capable of it. If a dog struggles or doesn't enjoy it, concentrate on something he can do instead. Don't pursue something he dislikes, as he will lose motivation or become unhappy.

Through, between, and around

Here you will find a selection of moves that are very useful to choreograph into your dance routines. They can be used as linking moves to join one move to another, or to quickly get your dog into position and ready for the next move.

THROUGH

Teaching a dog to go through your legs is a useful linking move. Your dog must know how to do this before he can leg weave (see page 44).

1 Stand in front of your dog, positioning your feet so that he can fit through your legs easily. Put a treat down a couple of inches behind you, then ask the dog to get it. Click as he goes through your legs but before he gets the treat.

2 Gradually place the treat farther behind until the dog eventually goes all the way through your legs to retrieve it. Click as he goes through. If he goes around instead, place the treat closer to you, holding it if necessary until he comes through.

3 Repeat in the other direction. Continue doing this, jumping around and getting the dog to retrieve the treat by going through your legs. Add the command "through" before you click and reward.

BETWEEN

In this move, the dog stands between your legs and maintains this position as you dance together.

1 Stand with your back to your dog, with your feet apart. Call the dog to come through your legs, then click while he is halfway through and give him a treat. Repeat, building in the command "between."

2 Soon, you can send him from the front to go around the back and through your legs when you say "between."

TRAINER'S TIP
🐾 "Between" can be developed into an on-the-spot circle. Hold a lure in your hand and slowly move it around you as you turn in place in either direction. Start with one or two steps before building into a complete circle. Click and treat when the dog moves around with you.

AROUND

For this move, the dog circles around one of your legs as you lure him with both of your hands.

1 Begin on the left side. Hold a button clicker in your right hand and treats in both hands, ready to lure your dog.

2 Standing with your left leg out, use a treat or toy to lure the dog in front of you and between your legs. Click as soon as he goes through your legs. Swap the hand you lure with to bring him all the way back to where he started. Give him the treat. At first, you will need to bend quite low, but as he becomes more proficient, you can straighten up until you are completely upright.

3 Practice several times, reducing the amount of luring and clicking and treating at different points of the circle to encourage a flowing move. Build in the verbal command "through, around" to mark the behavior.

FIGURE EIGHTS

Once your dog has mastered circling your leg, you can teach him to make a figure eight. The dog should learn figure eights while you are stationary and then progress to doing them while you walk. Play some upbeat music and move in time to it.

1 Hold a button clicker in your right hand and treats in both hands. Stand with your feet wide enough apart for your dog to weave through your legs easily. Position him on your left side, then bend forward and lure with your left hand around the front of your left leg. Swap hands so that he follows the treat in your right hand, which is behind your right knee. This will encourage him to go through your legs.

2 When the dog has gone through your legs, continue luring with your right hand around your right leg. Lure slowly, or the dog may cut corners to get the treat. Go back to your left hand, which is behind your left knee, to encourage the dog to go back through. Click as he passes under. When the dog has completed the figure eight, give him the treat.

3 Encourage flow and continuity by varying the timing of clicks and treats. Add the verbal command "weave" just before clicking. As you reduce the number of treats and your dog follows your hand signals, begin to stand upright.

Leg weaving

When leg weaving, the dog weaves back and forth through your legs as you walk along. While he is doing this, you should walk tall, keeping your head up, eyes forward, and hands down at your sides. Your dog should have learned the figure-eight weaving (see page 43) while you stand in place before attempting leg weaves. If he hasn't, you will have to walk in an awkward bent-over position to lure him. Not a good idea!

BASIC LEG WEAVES

When you teach your dog leg weaving, your strides should be purposeful and distinct, lifting the leg up quite high (but not so much that it resembles goose-stepping) to allow the dog to move easily through and under. Exaggerate your steps more in the early stages of training and then make them more natural later, varying the rhythm. Put on some marching music and use the tempo of the four-beat rhythm to help you develop the exercise.

1 Begin by putting your dog in the heelwork position on your left side. Now lift your right leg up and give the command "weave." As your dog passes under the right leg, start to move forward. When your right foot touches the ground, give the command "weave" again to encourage your dog to come back under the other leg.

2 This time, lift your left leg and click as your dog passes underneath it. When he is back on your left side, give him a treat.

3 Keep practicing this move, gradually building up the number of steps you take before clicking and offering your dog a treat.

Keyhole leg weaving

This variation is used in the Cancan routine (see page 92). Standing in place, lift one leg at a time, bend it at the knee, and place the foot against the side of your other leg. Give the "weave" command so that the dog threads through the keyhole gap, then repeat on the other side.

DANCE WEAVING

In this variation, you move from side to side. As you get better, you can dance from side to side, as seen in Match of the Day (see page 86). The rhythm for dance weaving is 1-2-3-kick to the right and 1-2-3-kick to the left, so the dog weaves on every fourth beat.

1 Put the dog in "close" and raise your right leg up in front, giving the "weave" command so that the dog passes under it. As he does, swing your right leg across in front of your left leg.

2 Step sideways with your left leg and cross your right leg over the left again. Now lift your leg for the dog to go under. Repeat in the opposite direction, maintaining the 1-2-3-kick rhythm.

REVERSE DANCE WEAVING

In this difficult move, the dog reverses back in a weave through your legs (see below). Teach the move one step at a time and have treats in both hands.

1 With the dog in "close" on your left side, put your left leg forward. Use the lure in your left hand to press him backward between your legs so that his back end goes between your legs first and he ends in "close," with his head at your right knee (this is the "side" command).

2 Step back with your left leg and use the lure in your right hand to press the dog backward so that his back end goes through your legs and he finishes back where he started, in the heelwork position on the left side.

3 Click as the dog backs through your legs, then give the treat when the move is complete and he is back in the "side" or "close" position. Build in a command such as "verse" (short for "reverse") to mark the move.

TRAINER'S TIP

🐾 The reverse weave is tricky with large dogs, as you must take big steps backward to get over the dog. However, if your dog is medium-sized, you can try this.

Creepy crawlies

Audiences love to see dogs creep in a routine. Visually, it's different to look at, since the dog stays close to the ground as he moves along. It is a good idea to combine moves from as many visual aspects as possible in a routine to give the audience more to look at. A few creeping moves, followed by some upright moves, can be stunning.

THE CREEP

The creep is physically demanding for dogs, especially if they have joint problems, so make sure your dog has a clean bill of health before trying this. The physical limitations of some larger breeds may mean they can only manage a half-creep, with their front end down and their hindquarters raised. Teaching the creep before the rollover (see page 48) avoids confusion.

1 Sit on the floor and raise your knees up in front of you. Put your dog in an upright "down" position at your side (see page 23), with his nose facing the direction of your knees. Use a treat to lure him through your legs while repeating the "down" command. Since your knees are in the way, he will not be able to stand and should creep through. Repeat several times, and click as he moves under your legs. Throw him the treat as he comes through to encourage him to complete the move.

2 The next stage is to put your dog in an upright "down" position once more, but this time you should remain on your feet and bend down to hold a treat to his nose. Try to get his nose slightly off the ground and his head parallel to the floor. Slowly move the food away from the dog, but keep saying "down." Click for the slightest effort that he makes to move forward, and give him the treat. As he begins to understand what you are asking him to do and responds accordingly, you can start to add in the command "creep" or "crawl" after you say "down."

3 Gradually extend the distance that the dog creeps by withholding the click, and reward a little at a time so that he creeps further each time. Eventually you can dispense with the word "down," and the dog should understand what is required simply from your use of the command "creep" or "crawl."

TRAINER'S TIP

🐾 To make it comfortable for the dog, teach "creep" on carpet. Use a high-value treat and hold it so that the dog's nose is only 2–3 inches off the ground. Move the treat slowly but surely so that he isn't tempted to snatch or to remain stationary.

CREEPING BACKWARD

This is harder to teach than the forward creep, and the dog's hindquarters will naturally raise off the ground to make the movement, so that it looks like he is walking backward in a bow. Teach it by putting the dog into "down" and, with a treat in your hand held close to his muzzle, gently but firmly push him back. Click as soon as he begins to move backward. Do this slowly and carefully to keep him from jumping up into a standing position. Gradually build the command "creep back" and dispense with the treat.

CREEPING LEG WEAVE

In this impressive move, the dog weaves through your legs while down on his haunches. Wait until your dog is proficient at doing ordinary leg weaving before asking him to try this move.

1 Put the dog in a "down" position, and as you move your left leg forward, your leg position will begin to cue the dog for the weave. Hold a treat down low to keep the dog down, and gradually lure him through the weave.

2 Click and treat for just a step or two at first, gradually building the number of steps until the dog understands and can confidently creep and weave.

3 Build in the verbal commands "creep" and "weave," and as the dog gets more confident, you can stop luring and stand more upright.

Combining the creep with rollovers (see page 48) or adding a "face" command (see pages 36–37) so that your dog stops and puts one or both paws over his face can look very effective in a routine.

Rollover and play dead

The rollover is a fun move, and most dogs love doing it. Once you've successfully taught the move, it may be better to minimize your practice sessions or you may find your dog is offering to do rollovers at every opportunity! Playing dead is a spectacular move in which you pretend to shoot the dog, who drops to the ground, apparently lifeless.

ROLLOVER

This move is taught by breaking it down into sections, clicking at every stage. The timing of the clicks is important. Aim to mark the rollover as soon as the dog's balance has reached the point of return.

1 Begin this move by teaching your dog to do a rollover onto his left side. Kneel down in front of the dog, who should be in the "down" position. Hold a treat out in your right hand, close to his nose. Then move the treat around and over your dog's head. This will turn his nose toward his shoulder.

2 Continue luring slowly around until the dog loses his balance and flops down onto his side into a flat "down" position. Click as soon as he is lying flat and give him the treat when his head is on the ground.

3 Put another treat in your hand and continue to lure him, moving your hand clockwise, turning your dog's head toward his side and up toward his shoulder. This

movement will bring his hind legs around, and he will roll over onto his other side. Once fully rolled over, click, and while he is on the ground, give him the treat.

4 Use another treat to lure your dog back into the "down" position. Take your time and keep practicing these steps before you try to achieve the rollover in one move. As your dog begins to understand, you should build in the "rollover" command before you click and treat.

TRAINER'S TIPS

❧ If your dog struggles to roll from the flat "down" on one side onto his other side, help him by lifting the front paw nearest the floor.

❧ Practice the rollovers on both sides, but be careful to lure with the correct hand, or you could have difficulty stretching around and make the rollover difficult for your dog to achieve.

PLAYING DEAD

The quicker your dog drops down and the stiller he is, the better this move looks. Most audiences are not too keen on seeing a handler shoot their dog, so in the Viva España! routine (see page 101) the dog is "brought back to life" and takes his revenge. The audience always appreciates the humor of this role reversal.

1 Give the "rollover" command, but when the dog is halfway over, tell him to "wait," then click and treat. Practice several times, gradually lengthening the time the dog waits before you click and reward.

2 If you prefer the dog to drop on his side rather than his back, ask for the rollover and click just before or after he has rolled into the flat "down" position. Give the treat when his head is on the floor. Practice several times and build in a command, such as "dead," before clicking.

3 It looks dramatic if the dog stretches his paws out while "dead." While he is in "wait" in step 1, ask him to touch your hand. When his paw touches, click and reward. As the dog begins to understand, build in the commands "dead" and "wait" just before you click. Soon you will be able to drop the earlier commands of "rollover" and "wait."

4 Finally, position the dog in front, and give the verbal command "dead." He should immediately fall into position. If not, go back to the previous stages, adding the commands of "rollover" and "wait," until he understands what you want him to do.

5 Give your release signal of "OK" to bring your dog miraculously back to life!

PERFORMANCE NOTES

🐾 To make this look dramatic, practice until the move is cued by you holding a toy gun or shaping your fingers into a gun and pointing at the dog.

EYE CONTACT

To get your dog to close his eyes as he plays dead, kneel next to him and stroke gently between his eyes. This should relax him so much that he closes them. As soon as they close, click and reward. Gradually extend the time he keeps his eyes shut by withholding the click.

Alternatively, simply leave him until he naturally relaxes and shuts his eyes. As soon as he does, click and give a reward. Although the dog will open his eyes when he hears the click, he will soon realize that he is being clicked and rewarded for closing them.

Take a bow

What better finale to your routine than you and your dog taking a bow together! You can use it as a final pose in its own right or as a way of acknowledging the audience's applause. The bow can also be used as a very effective opening pose.

THE BOW POSITION

The idea of the bow is for the dog to keep his hindquarters up in the air while at the same time lowering his forelegs down and back from his front paws. The dog should look as if he is going into the "down" position but has stopped just before his hindquarters lower to the floor. If you have already taught the upright "down" position (see page 23), you will notice that the dog goes into a bow when his front end goes down.

Using the clicker

When teaching the bow, you need to be very accurate with the clicker. It is crucial that you click just before the dog is fully committed to the full "down" position. Clicking too late will mean the dog thinks you are rewarding him for the "down" position rather than the halfway pose you are after.

TEACHING THE BOW

There are a couple of ways of teaching the bow, the simplest being to tell the dog to go into the "down" position and clicking just as the dog lowers his front legs but before he drops into a full "down" position. The problem with this method is that you must be very confident about using the clicker accurately, or you will not be able to capture that exact moment you need. For someone relatively inexperienced, it may be better to use a treat to lure the dog and break the move down into sections as follows.

1 Kneel down in front of the dog, who should be facing you in the "in front" position. Hold the treat you are going to offer in the underhand position, so that he can see and smell it but can't snatch it away.

2 Very carefully push the treat toward the dog but keep it slightly down, at about a forty-five-degree angle. Imagine that you are trying to push the treat between your dog's front legs in order to bring his nose down and back. This will change the dog's point of balance so that it is easier for him to drop down onto his forelegs. As soon as you see him lower his forelegs, click and give him the treat. Make sure you click before he drops into a full "down" position.

3 Develop the move by delaying the click for a little longer each time, as this will encourage the dog to drop down lower. You are trying to get the dog to drop down onto his elbows but keep his back end up in the air. Practice the exercise several times until the dog can complete the move and begins to understand exactly what you want from him.

4 Now you can start to build in a verbal command. Use the word "bend" or "stretch" rather than the word "bow," which can sound slightly similar to the word "down" and could be confusing. You can also add on the word "wait" to lengthen the time of the bow, but you should eventually be able to drop this.

5 When the dog is able to bow from the verbal command, try it with you standing up. Wait until the dog has gone into a bow and then bow to him, or try to bow toward each other simultaneously. Remember, this is for a dance routine, so give your bow some finesse by putting one hand behind your back and using your other hand to give some dramatic emphasis to the move.

PERFORMANCE NOTES

🐾 In heelwork to music routines, you can use the bow with props. For example, you could position a child's bucket or a small basket in front of your dog and then ask him to hold it in his mouth as he takes a bow. Another idea would be to have the dog holding a hat in his mouth so that he can take a bow while holding it and then bring it to the handler, who can take it from him and put it on her head with a flourish.

Twists and turns

Your dog should look as if he's almost chasing his tail when he's performing the twist well. Smaller or medium-sized dogs find this move very easy, but larger, heavyweight dogs will naturally struggle to get the same speed or effect, although it can still look very dramatic.

THE TWIST

Your hands will signal to the dog which direction you want him to twist, so it is very important that you use the correct hand to lure the dog on both sides. If you imagine swimming the breaststroke, you will recall that the right hand always circles in a clockwise direction, while the left hand always circles counterclockwise. If you can remember this, you will never be confused about which hand to use.

1 Put the dog in the "in front" position. Have a treat ready in your right hand, and start to lure his head around to the right. Once his nose has reached as far back as his shoulder, click and give him the treat. Get another treat and repeat the lure, but this time take it further so that the dog's nose is close to his tail. When he takes a step with his front feet, click and give him the treat.

2 For the next stage, continue to lure your dog's nose past the tail position so that he now has to step right around with his front and hind legs. Click when he reaches the halfway mark, and reward him when he is back facing you.

3 Practice this several times until the dog is able to complete a full circle in one easy, flowing move. Remember to click just as he passes the halfway point and reward him as he faces you again. It won't be long before you can dispense with the lure of the treats and the dog will simply follow your hand. When he can do that, build in the command "twist" just before you click and treat. Ultimately, you will even be able to dispense with the hand signals, as simply saying the word "twist" will send your dog into a spin!

TRAINER'S TIPS

🐾 Don't just stop at one twist. Encourage the dog to do several by delaying the moment you click to when he has done one-and-a-half twists, then two twists, then two-and-a-half twists, and so on.

🐾 When you are teaching the dog to twist in the opposite direction, don't forget to lure with your other hand. (Remember the breaststroke!) In addition, give that direction a different verbal command from the other side. For example, use the word "twist" for clockwise and "spin" for counterclockwise.

ROUTINES WITH A TWIST

The twist is a move that features many times in the routines in this book—for example, in Saturday Night Fever (see page 95)—but you can build twists into almost any routine if the music is appropriate. Once your dog has mastered twisting, practice it with music and walk alongside him, asking him to twist as you are walking. Try single twists, or double them up so that you do a few steps of walking or circling together and then twist or spin the dog in time to the music. Have some fun and try to get the dog to twist on either side of you, or both of you twisting around together.

Merry-go-round

In the Mack and Mabel routine on page 119, you send your dog out on a large circle so that he is running around you. This move can also be useful when there is more than one dog working in a routine. You can have one or two dogs working in close and the other dog or dogs out on a larger circle.

CIRCLING AROUND

Begin by teaching the dog to circle closely around you. The trick to doing this successfully is being quick to transfer the lure. Any hesitations or confusions will distract the dog and spoil the move. It is useful to practice transferring the lure from hand to hand in front and behind in both directions before you start working with the dog. If your fingers are not as flexible as they might be or you find it difficult to transfer the lure, you could try putting a treat in each hand.

1 With the dog in the left heelwork position, hold a treat or toy, plus the clicker, in your right hand and lure the dog across the front of you, around your right side. As you bring the dog around to the back, switch the lure to the other hand so that you can keep him moving around. As soon as the dog is following your left hand, toward the left side of your body, click. Wait until the dog has completed the circle and returned to the original heelwork position at your side before you give him the treat.

2 Practice this several times. Always click after you have transferred the lure, but begin to offer treats at different points on the circle, not just at the heelwork position. Build in the word "around," and gradually dispense with the lure. Your dog should follow your hand movements, although once he has learned the verbal command, you can dispense with the hand signals as well.

3 Practice this exercise in both directions, being careful to use the opposite hand sequence. Give the counterclockwise "around" command a different name, such as "circle," so that the dog doesn't get confused.

OUT ON A CIRCLE

This move is taught with you standing in a puppy pen, which acts as a see-through barrier between you and the dog. If you want to teach the dog to do very large circles, you can use two puppy pens linked together.

1 Once you are standing in the puppy pen, take a treat and lure your dog around the circumference of the pen. As your dog begins to follow, throw some treats in front of him every two or three strides. Click as he moves forward to get the treats but just before he reaches them. Do this several times and begin to build in a verbal command such as "go out" before you click and throw the dog a treat.

2 The next stage is to remain standing in the middle of the pen and turn in place, giving the verbal command and throwing out food treats to keep the movement going. Once the dog is moving well, reduce and vary how many treats you throw out. It is not knowing whether he will get a treat for half a circle, one circle, or two circles that will motivate the dog to keep circling around you.

3 Once your dog is able to circle around you from the verbal command "go out," you can dispense with the puppy pen. Give the command again, and as soon as he starts to circle around you, throw treats out to keep him circling wide.

4 Practice the move in both directions, and choose a separate command to mark this, such as "wide" instead of "go out."

TRAINER'S TIP

🐾 If your dog starts to circle close to you, throw a treat out to move him further away again and click just before he reaches it. If he continues to come in close, put the puppy pen back and practice with it a few more times before trying again.

Pole dancing

Don't worry, this type of pole dancing won't make you blush! Now that your dog has learned to do circles around you, he will be able to circle around a pole or prop. Introducing your dog to pole work opens up many more possibilities for your routines, since eventually you can have him running around the pole, going over or under it, or even carrying the pole in his mouth.

LEARNING TO POLE DANCE

Your dog should have very few problems learning to do this. When teaching, use a lightweight pole that stands securely in a cone so that you don't have to worry about it wobbling around or falling over as you try to lure the dog around it. Later, you can use an umbrella, a walking stick, or any other kind of prop you want the dog to go around. Pole dancing is used in the Top Hat and Tails routine (see page 107), where the dog circles around a cane.

1 Position the dog and the pole so that they are both on the right side of you. Choose a high-value toy or treat—a toy may be seen more easily. Holding the lure in your hand, lure the dog away from you and around the far side of the pole. Click just before he completes a full circle and then give him a reward. Practice this several times, increasing the number of circles you ask for before you click and reward.

2 As your dog becomes more competent at circling, gradually stop luring but hold the toy or treat still on top of the pole. Use the command "pole" to mark one direction and "circle pole" to mark the other. The dog should circle the pole in a counterclockwise direction on the right and a clockwise direction on the left.

PERFORMANCE NOTE

❧ In a routine, you will often see the handler holding a cane and the dog circling close to it in one direction while the handler circles farther out in the opposite direction. This looks very effective and is best practiced first with the cane standing in a cone. Hold the cane firmly and keep it straight when you are doing circle work around it, as this looks tidier than if it is leaning over at an angle.

WEAVING WITH A CANE

Once your dog understands the concept of going around the pole in both directions, you can introduce some variations, like a figure eight. This is a move that can be incorporated into the Top Hat and Tails routine (see page 107).

1 Use two freestanding poles for this, spaced an arm's length away from you on each side so that you can reach past both ends of the poles with a lure.

2 Stand in the middle of the two poles but slightly back. With your dog on your left, lure him with your left hand clockwise around the left pole. The verbal command for this should be either "pole" or "circle pole."

3 As the dog returns, lure him across the front of you and swap the lure into your right hand. Use the opposite verbal command as the dog circles the right pole.

4 When your dog returns, lure him back around the other side of you by swapping the lure into your left hand. Click and reward when the dog reaches the starting point at your left heel.

5 Keep practicing until you no longer have to lure but can simply place the lure hand on top of the pole you want him to circle.

When your dog understands to circle whichever pole your hand is on, you can develop the move further. Hold a cane in your right hand and give the command "pole," so that the dog knows to circle it. As he completes the circle, swap the cane into your left hand and place it on the left side of your body. Just before you put the pole down, give the opposite verbal command for him to circle in that direction.

TRAINER'S TIP
🐾 Keep practicing this, and you will soon see that the move has a rhythm to it. Put some music on and practice again, swaying a little from side to side as you pick up and put down the cane. You will soon be able to dispense with verbal commands.

Walk back and back up

Reverse movements can be used to develop many of the basic moves your dog has already learned and make them look even more dramatic. Reverse weaving and reverse circling look particularly impressive, and audiences love these moves.

WALK BACK

Begin by teaching the dog to walk backward in a straight line away from you. There are a couple of ways to teach this, but when teaching small dogs, the first method is very useful, as they naturally have to reverse back a few steps to get you in their vision.

1 Ask the dog to stand in front, keeping your feet wide enough apart for the dog to fit between them. Place a treat on the ground between your feet, and invite the dog to take it. When the dog has eaten it, he will inevitably step back and look up to see if there are any more treats. Click this backward step and reward him with another treat placed between your feet. Keep doing this until the dog begins to understand that he is being rewarded for the step back.

2 Now try delaying the click. Your dog will probably reverse to the same point as before, stopping as he anticipates the click. When the click doesn't come, he should step back again. When he does, click and put another reward down. Build in the verbal command "walk back," and slowly dispense with putting the treat down between your feet.

If you prefer, try this more hands-on method:

1 Ask the dog to stand in front of you. Hold a treat in the underhand position close to his nose. Use the treat hand to push gently but firmly into your dog's muzzle to encourage him to tuck his head back into his neck. If you push too slowly, he may sit down or refuse to move, so make the movement decisive and firm. Ensure that your hand is not too high, or his head will come up and he may sit down; equally, if your hand is too low, he may lie down.

2 Take a step toward the dog, and he should take a step backward. As soon as he does, click and give him the treat. Keep practicing until the dog begins to get the idea that you want him to go back. Now begin to build in the verbal command "walk back" just before you click and reward.

BACK UP BETWEEN YOUR LEGS

You can now teach your dog to back up between your legs. There are quite a few components and commands for him to learn, so take each stage slowly. If he appears confused at any point, simply go back to the stage he last understood and start again.

1 Begin by standing astride the dog, and while holding a treat to his nose, gently push him back. Click as he steps back, and reward him when he returns to your side. Practice this until he can do it without the push, and build in the command "back up."

2 Gradually increase the distance between you and your dog, clicking each time he reverses back through your legs and rewarding him each time he gets back to your side. Develop the move by asking him to "stand, wait," then walk behind him and ask him to back up.

3 Teach him to do a half turn by luring him with a treat, clicking when he is facing away from you so that the behavior is marked at that point. Build in the command "turn," and when he has learned to do this, you can link all the moves together. Soon your dog will be able to "walk back," "turn," and finally "back up" through your legs. The crowds love it!

TRAINER'S TIP

🐾 If your dog keeps backing into you, reposition your legs to help him get through easily. It is difficult for a dog to see behind him without turning his head, but if you keep saying "back up," it will help him locate you.

Going in reverse

Your dance routines would be fairly limited if you and your dog were only able to move together in a forward direction. It's important to demonstrate that you are able to move together in any direction, including sideways or in a circle. The tighter your dog manages to stick to you, the more polished and professional your routine will look.

WALKING BACK TOGETHER

It is easiest to teach this move using a puppy pen. Use a wall as one barrier and the folded-out puppy pen as the other side, so that you and your dog can work in the tunnel you have formed.

1 Put your dog in the left heelwork position and hold a treat toward his nose. Now take a single step back and push the treat into the dog's muzzle so that he too takes a step back. Click and reward him with a treat for the step back.

2 Repeat this move several times more, and gradually increase the number of steps you take backward before clicking and rewarding your dog. As your dog begins to understand what you are asking him to do, you can add in the verbal command "close back" or "heel back." When he can walk back with you for about ten feet, you are at the stage where you can begin to practice without the use of the barriers. Go back to using the barriers if the dog starts to wander away, move out to the side, or get too far behind you.

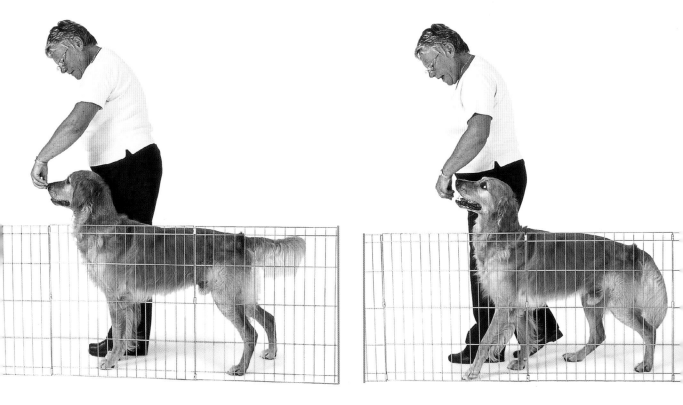

REVERSING AROUND

You can develop the reversing move further by teaching the dog to do a backward circle around you. The dog needs to keep as tight as possible to the handler as he reverses round. Use the puppy pen again, this time shaping it into a close circle around you. If you don't have a pen, improvise by using the corner of a room and a chair as a barrier. Ideally, there should only be enough space for you to stand in the middle of the puppy pen while the dog moves around you. The idea is that the pen will prevent the dog from walking back and encourage him to circle around you.

1 Put your dog in the heelwork position on the left side, then give him the command "back," but this time stay still. If he hesitates, you can encourage him with a treat, pushed gently into his muzzle. Click and reward the dog as he starts to walk backward around you. Break down the move by clicking as the dog comes past your right leg, then again as he completes half of the circle.

2 Gradually build up to the full circle before clicking, then click intermittently as the dog completes several circles. You can build in a verbal command, such as "reverse" (some people shorten this to "verse").

3 Once your dog begins to understand what you want him to do and he is circling confidently around you, you can dispense with the pen and try doing this move in an open space. As always, if he starts to wander away from you, put the pen back into position and practice inside again. He needs to learn that the circle must be made closely around you.

4 Take your time and wait until the dog can circle confidently and tightly on command before you start teaching him to do the move in the opposite direction. Some people use a different command to mark the change of direction, but I find I don't have to because my dogs are cued by whether or not they are in the "close" or "side" position.

Jumping

Jumping over or through props really shows off your dog's agility and adds another visual element to a routine.

BASIC JUMPING

When you create a jump for your dog, put it as low as two inches from the ground. This will encourage the dog to go over the obstacle rather than crawl under it.

1 Position the dog in front of the obstacle, telling him to wait. Once you are on the other side, turn to face the dog. Hold your arms open and call enthusiastically. Click as he jumps, and reward when he gets to you. Repeat several times, building in the command "over."

2 If the dog swerves around the jump, reposition him closer and consider lowering the pole. Don't continue if he persistently refuses to jump—there may be a physical explanation for this. Get him checked by a veterinarian before continuing.

3 Develop the exercise by placing a treat down in front of the obstacle. Return to your dog, giving the release command "OK." Run at the side, clicking as he jumps over. Repeat several times, then let him go alone.

4 Finally, ask the dog to jump an obstacle with no treat in front of it, rewarding intermittently after he has performed several jumps on command.

5 Sit down with your legs stretched out. Place a treat on the far side of your legs and give the "over" command. Click as he jumps and repeat in both directions.

JUMPING INTO A BASKET

If you are working with a small dog, you can teach him to jump into a wicker shopping basket. You can encourage this during free time play (see pages 66–67) or simply throw a treat or a toy into the basket and click as the dog steps in to retrieve it while giving the command "in it."

> ### PERFORMANCE NOTE
> 🐾 Use less jumping in your routines as a dog ages. Even large, athletic dogs should not be asked to jump higher than 2½ feet. Don't ask him to jump anything dangerous—no hoops of fire!

JUMPING OVER AN ARM

You will need a helper to teach your dog to jump over an arm. Ask the helper to kneel with her arm outstretched.

1 Tell the dog to "wait," and hold a treat in front of his nose. Keep slightly ahead of the dog as you release him and command "over." Run at the side as he jumps, clicking as he goes over and rewarding him as he gets to you. Repeat several times, with the helper gradually raising her arm to shoulder height.

2 Stand behind your helper, telling your dog to "wait" in front of her outstretched arm. Hold a treat out and give the "over" command, clicking as the dog jumps and rewarding him as he gets to you.

3 Now you can dispense with your helper. Kneel down a few paces away from your dog with your arm held out and give the "over" command. Click as he jumps over and throw a reward out for him. Repeat in both directions.

JUMPING THROUGH YOUR ARMS

Once more, you will need a willing assistant to help you teach this move.

1 Hold a hoop upright and ask your dog to walk through. Click when his front half is through, and reward when the rest follows. Repeat, gradually raising the hoop higher. Now start throwing a treat out for him, adding the command "hoop." This should soon be unnecessary, as the sight of the hoop will signal the move.

2 With the dog in "sit and wait," bend down and hold your arms out in a low circle in front of you. Ask your helper to stand on the other side of you with a treat. Give the "hoop" command and click as the dog jumps through. The helper should throw the reward a few paces in front of the dog. Gradually increase the height of the circle, clicking as your dog jumps up and through.

3 Now try on your own. Place a treat on the floor, hold your arms in a circle, and give the "hoop" command. Your dog should soon use your arm position as a visual cue, and you can drop the verbal command.

JUMPING INTO ARMS

Ask the dog to "sit" and "wait," and stand far enough away from him so he has room for a run-up. If he is small, you could kneel so that he won't have to jump as high. Call him and pat your chest, giving the command "up." Click as the dog jumps up and then catch him. Ask bigger dogs to jump up into a chair or sofa instead, clicking as they jump and catching them before they get to the furniture. The dog should jump as soon as you give the visual signal or the "up" command.

POP UP!

Small dogs often jump up with all four legs off the ground. Most do this naturally as they play, and you can mark this behavior by clicking and treating, building in the command "pop." To teach the jump from scratch, hold a toy or treat over the dog's head and invite him to get it. Click as he jumps up, then give the treat, building in the "pop" command.

Targeted moves

On pages 26 and 27, we looked at examples of target work, where the dog learned the importance of following your hand or a target stick. Now we will progress this area of your dog's training by developing targeting into more advanced moves using the props featured in some of the routines. Targeted moves form an integral part of heelwork to music, as they link together other moves and help your routines to flow effortlessly.

TARGET PRACTICE

Using a metal target stick, with a toy or foam ball on the end, gives you much greater scope than just using your hand. The target or prop becomes a visual signal, and the extra length of the stick enables you to ask your dog for more distance or height. When the dog is targeting a stick, you can use it as a directional tool to cue different moves. You can also use it as an alternative training method for some of the other moves in the book, such as "down," the bow, or standing tall.

Get the low down

Lower the target stick down between the dog's two front legs. Your dog will naturally follow the direction of the stick with his nose, his head will come down, and his back end will lift up. From this position, it is easy to encourage him to go into a "down" or a bow by building in the relevant verbal command.

Standing tall

Stand in front of the dog and hold the target stick up high in the air so that the dog's head comes up. To continue targeting the stick, he will have to lift both front legs off the ground (in a beg position), and if you continue to raise the target stick he should stand tall on his back legs. Build in the verbal command "both" to help mark the move.

Figure eights

Hold the stick out in front of you or to the side so that the dog targets it on a circle or makes sweeping figure eights around you and the target stick. Now hold the target stick out in front as you walk along and move it in large, sweeping loops from side to side while giving the "pat" command. Your dog will do a more unusual slalom-type movement, where his head remains in the same direction but his body bends in serpentine loops as he moves across the room.

USING A TARGET PROP

Once your dog understands the principle of targeting, it is a natural progression to dispense with the target stick and introduce a more interesting prop, such as an umbrella, cane, or magic wand.

High-step trot

Use the "nose" or "pat" command (see page 26) to ask the dog to target a prop, such as a cane or umbrella. Walk quickly so that the dog's pace increases to a brisk trot. Because the dog is nose targeting, he will naturally focus his attention up toward the prop. Hold the prop high so that his head and nose are up (but not so high that it is uncomfortable for him), and as you do so, you will be able to regulate his pace and create and control a much more dynamic, high-stepping trot that audiences will adore.

Creeping

Here's an alternative way of teaching the creep move described on page 46.

Hold a target prop such as a cane down toward the ground to lower the dog's body. If necessary, you can also give the "down" command. Continue to hold the prop down, close to the dog's nose. Give the "nose" or "pat" command to encourage him to target the prop. Now start to walk backward away from the dog. He will start to creep along the ground as he continues to focus on the prop.

Time to experiment

There are many possibilities with targeting for you to explore and enjoy. Try planting a target prop (such as a walking stick or cane) down in front of you so that the dog can weave or circle around it. The dog can target or follow a prop in all directions, and this gives you many more possibilities within a routine. When done properly, the dog is so focused on the target prop that it's almost as if he is attached to an invisible leash that you are leading him around with. Take some time to experiment and practice with a target stick, and you will be amazed at how useful a tool this is.

TRAINER'S TIP

🐾 A foam ball is easy for a dog to see, but if your dog is motivated by food, you can try putting a tasty treat, such as a piece of cheese or sausage, on the end of the target stick. Alternatively, rub a piece of chicken over the ball so that the dog can smell it.

Free time

During free time, you give your dog the opportunity to be creative and see what he offers to do for you, instead of you telling your dog what you want him to do. Free time is a lot of fun for you and the dog, and it can be done either with props or without. It gives a break from formal training and is particularly useful in heelwork to music, as the dog may come up with ideas for prop use that you would perhaps not have considered.

LEARNING FROM FREE TIME

When your dog uses a prop in new ways during free time, you can capture the actions with a clicker and later choreograph them into one of your routines. Because the clicker is such a clever and versatile tool, it encourages this kind of interactive communication between you and the dog. Think of the clicker as a kind of invisible camera that you can use to zoom in on a particular behavior you would like to "capture" for future use in a routine.

Natural behavior

All dogs will naturally use their nose, feet, and mouth to explore or investigate new objects. However, they are often discouraged from doing this by owners who perhaps don't want them to put their paws on the furniture, so the dog will gradually lose this natural exploratory behavior. Free time will encourage the dog to have fun, be inquisitive, lose his inhibitions, and try out new things. The more experienced your dog becomes at heelwork to music, the better he will become at free time, and you will be amazed at what he tries to do to please you.

FREE TIME IDEAS

Begin by selecting a prop—perhaps something the dog is fairly unfamiliar with, such as a plastic bucket, a wicker shopping basket, or a footstool.

1 Put the prop down in the middle of the room and sit down next to it with a container of treats. Your dog will soon begin to associate this with free time.

2 Sit or stand quietly, and watch as the dog uses his paw, nose, or mouth to explore the object. Ignore any behavior you don't like, but click and reward any that you do. It may be picking up the bucket in his teeth, jumping into the basket, or placing one or both feet on the table or footstool. All you have to do is wait to see what the dog does.

3 Mark any behavior that you like with a command, such as "pick it up," "in it," or "on it," but be careful not to use words that may confuse your dog in the future.

4 If, after a few minutes, the dog is not offering you any new behavior, try changing your position, perhaps by kneeling or sitting down rather than standing over him. This can encourage new responses.

FREE TIME IN ACTION

In this training session, we put down a small plastic table that Gypsy had never seen before and observed what types of behavior she would offer. All of these behaviors were clicked and rewarded, and may be seen in future routines!

Gypsy began by putting both front paws on the table . . .

... A freestanding cane was introduced, and Gypsy stood tall and put both paws on the cane . . . She then circled the cane, and when I tried to encourage new behaviors by kneeling down, Gypsy bowed to the cane . . .

. . . She then jumped up onto the table and sat down . . .

. . . A ball was introduced, and Gypsy nudged it along with her nose and then stood with her front paws on the ball . . .

. . . After a couple of minutes, Gypsy circled the table, jumped back on, and stood with all four feet on it . . .

. . . A cowboy hat further aroused Gypsy's curiosity, and she decided to stand on top of it.

Putting a routine together

Planning the basics

Before you begin to think about the moves, props, or costumes in your routine, you need to plan the basics, such as the music and the venue. These elements will have a strong influence on the mood and moves in your routine.

MOOD

Consider the following points when you are planning a performance with your dog.

🐾 What kind of mood do you want to create—humorous and uplifting, or more serious and thoughtful?

🐾 Who will your audience be?

🐾 What physical limitations and training does your dog have? Consider his build, age, and experience. Start with something simple and short, then add more elements to a routine as your dog's experience grows.

🐾 Clever choreography can change the mood of a routine. See page 103 for the surprise ending in Viva España!

VENUE

The venue and the space available to you will play a major part in the type of routine you are able to perform. You can always adapt a routine for a smaller venue, perhaps by cutting a section, or if the venue is large, you can build extra moves in. The most important thing is to make proper use of the space, so that the entire audience has a good view of what you and your dog are doing. If you are doing a demonstration, visit the venue beforehand to assess the size and shape of the performance area, the seating arrangements, and the lighting and music facilities. All of these will affect your performance in some way.

MUSIC

Your choice of music is of major importance. Marching tunes are good for beginners, since they have a rhythmic four-time beat. Choose music that is in two, four, or eight beats so that you can count out the steps. Remember to factor in your turns. For example, in the Stars and Stripes routine (see page 80), there are sequences of marching steps and about-faces. Count these as: "turn-2-3-4, turn-2-3-4, turn-2-3-4," instead of "1-2-3-4-turn, 1-2-3-4-turn," or you will soon be out of time with the music.

Lyrics

Some people prefer a song with lyrics to help them choreograph a routine. The Puppet on a String routine (see page 89) uses the lyrics of the 1960s British pop song by Sandie Shaw to mark where and when the dog moves. For example, the line, "I may win on the roundabout," is an ideal opportunity for your dog to circle around you on the word "roundabout" while you circle the other way.

If you opt for a well-known tune with a good beat, you can get the audience on your side. A compilation of Glenn Miller tunes is ideal for the Into the Swing routine (see page 122). As soon as the audience hears the opening chords, they will immediately start clapping along. Keep this in mind when selecting your music, as this could be a distraction for your dog or make you lose your confidence if you are inexperienced at performing in front of people. On the other hand, some enthusiastic clapping may help put you at ease!

Choosing music for your dog

Choose music that suits the look and personality of your dog. A toy poodle looks and moves very differently from a German shepherd, so try different music to discover what suits your dog best. If possible, ask someone to videotape you and the dog so that you can try out different moves and music. When you watch the video later, you will get a better idea of what works best.

WARNING
Be aware of copyright laws, and check with the relevant authorities to ensure that you have the appropriate licenses for playing your chosen music in public.

Props and costumes

The most important consideration when planning any show is to ensure that your dog is the star. Extremely flamboyant costumes or theatrical moves are not necessary because they will simply detract from your dog's performance.

CHOOSING PROPS

Sometimes a prop can immediately suggest a theme for a routine. For example, an umbrella obviously lends itself to the famous Gene Kelly dance sequence in the film *Singin' in the Rain* (see page 83). With less well known routines, you should think more carefully about what kinds of props you can introduce to bring ingenuity to the performance.

Props and your dog

Be inventive with props, but always consider how they will be viewed by your dog when they are used in a routine. Will the prop be too cumbersome or heavy? Will it always be fully visible? If not, you may have to modify the prop in some way. For example, in the Top Hat and Tails routine on page 107, a small lightweight dowel was used for the cane, so it was easy for the dog to carry. The dowel was painted black, and pieces of gold tape were fastened to both ends, so that the dog could easily see and target either end of the cane, depending on what the routine required.

PROP SUGGESTIONS

Here are some ideas for props that you might like to include in your routines:

- Skateboard
- Cane
- Top hat
- Magic wand
- Walking stick
- Hoop
- Kitchen mop
- Cummerbund
- Matador's cape
- Broomstick
- Soccer ball
- Chair
- Umbrella
- Fake bunch of flowers

RULES AND REGULATIONS

Governing bodies in different countries around the world all have slightly different rules about the use of props as well as what costumes are acceptable for the handler and dog, so check beforehand if you intend to compete. For demonstration purposes, of course, pretty much anything goes, provided you do not put the dog in any danger or ask him to work with a prop that causes him anxiety or physically impedes him in any way.

COSTUMES

You can have your costumes custom-made, but you do not need to go to this expense. You may have clothes hanging in your wardrobe that can easily be adapted by you—or by a friend who is handy with a sewing needle. Charity or thrift shops are another great source of costume material, as are garage and estate sales.

Costume tips

🐾 Consider renting a period costume for routines. I rented a G.I. costume for the Into the Swing routine (see page 122). As soon as I put it on, I felt like I was back in the dance halls of World War II, and it really helped get me in the mood.

🐾 Use any sparkly material left over from making a costume to make a matching collar for your dog.

🐾 Add inexpensive silver moon and stars earrings to your dogs' collars for the World of Magic routine (see page 116). They will shimmer under the lights effectively every time the dogs move and add to the magical atmosphere.

🐾 Choose clothes that will make you feel comfortable. If the thought of wearing a cancan outfit (see page 92) fills you with horror, then you could always choose something more conservative. Remember that the audience has come to see the dogs. There is no doubt, however, that a good costume will add a sense of theater and showmanship.

🐾 Whatever you choose to wear, make sure it is something that you are able to forget about during your routine. The last thing you want is to be worrying about tassels falling off or tripping over a hem.

🐾 Always have a dress rehearsal before your competition or demonstration so that you can modify or change any elements of the costumes or props that could potentially cause you problems.

🐾 Choose a costume that is lightweight and doesn't have flapping sleeves or pant legs that may hinder your dog or confuse the signals you give to him.

🐾 If you have long hair, tie it back out of the way so that it doesn't fall over your face or obscure your hand signals in any way.

Planning out on paper

Once you have selected the piece of music you wish to use and have chosen the theme of the routine that you and your dog are going to perform, the next important step is to plan your performance out on paper.

BE STAGE AWARE

First, do a sketch of the performance area and start to map out where and when you will do the moves. Aim to fill the whole stage, and if one section of the audience may find it difficult to see a particular move, repeat it more than once so that everyone has an opportunity to see properly. Many venues do not have tiered seating, so avoid performing close to the front row, as most of the audience will have difficulty seeing this.

TIMING

Most stereo systems have timers on them, so you can listen to the music and note when a section starts and finishes. Begin by timing the entire piece of music, then find the midpoint. Are there changes of tempo and mood within the piece? If so, change the mood of the routine, perhaps sending the dog out onto a big circle or bringing him in close for a high-trot sequence.

Think about your starting and finishing poses (see page 74) and calculate how long you need to hold them until the next move starts or the music finishes. Make good use of linking moves like "through" and "between" (see page 42) to help you get the dog into position, ready for the next part of your routine.

PLAN FOR STARS AND STRIPES ROUTINE

Some people like to map out their routine on paper using colored pens or pencils to code the various moves and directions, such as circles, figure eights, and walking back. Others prefer to simply write the entire routine out in full, like I have done for the Stars and Stripes routine that appears on page 80 (see plan, opposite).

Plan for Stars and Stripes Routine

1. Starting pose—Dog in "sit" at the side of the handler; dog and handler salute each other.

2. Forward for eight, dog creeping.

3. Turn right together and perform two in-place clockwise circles.

4. Walk forward for four and do two clockwise twists.

5. Walk backward for eight with dog creeping forward.

6. Dog does two clockwise in-place circles.

7. Handler and dog walk forward four; dog does two twists counterclockwise.

8. About-face for four, and dog does two twists clockwise.

9. Dog targets right hand as handler walks in a circle for sixteen beats.

10. Handler changes direction; dog targets left hand as handler walks in a circle for sixteen beats.

11. Handler does a counterclockwise circle in place, and dog circles around handler in the opposite direction for sixteen beats.

12. Handler does slower counterclockwise circle in place, and the dog reverses around handler in the opposite direction for sixteen beats.

13. Handler does high-step march in slow clockwise circle for sixteen beats with dog weaving through legs.

14. Handler stands in place, and dog weaves through one leg for sixteen beats.

15. Handler puts dog to heel and walks forward slowly for four beats.

16. Handler and dog turn in an in-place circle for four beats.

17. Handler walks back for eight with dog in heel position.

18. Handler and dog walk sideways to the left for eight beats, turn counterclockwise on the eighth beat, and walk sideways together again to the right for eight beats.

19. Handler turns counterclockwise, walks sideways right for two beats, twists the dog counterclockwise, walks sideways left for two beats, and twists the dog clockwise (so handler twists the dog in a figure eight).

20. Handler walks a clockwise circle for eight beats with dog targeting left hand.

21. Handler sends dog out onto a large circle where he canters around clockwise. Handler skips in a smaller counterclockwise circle.

22. Dog joins handler in front, and they both skip eight to the right and eight to the left two times.

23. Handler walks forward for eight beats; dog reverses and twists clockwise on the eighth beat.

24. Handler and dog reverse back for four beats; on the fourth beat, the dog goes through handler's legs.

25. Turn and repeat above move in the opposite direction.

26. Handler reverses for four beats; dog reverses in the opposite direction for four beats.

27. Dog does two clockwise twists and two counterclockwise twists.

28. Dog and handler do one clockwise circle together.

29. Dog and handler walk forward together for six beats and turn counterclockwise on beats seven–eight.

30. Handler walks forward with dog targeting left hand (on hip) for four beats, about-faces, walks forward for four beats, then about-faces again. (Do four of these, one in each corner of a large square.)

31. Dog and handler about-face again and march up the center line together.

32. Dog and handler perform an in-place turn and two counterclockwise turns.

33. Handler halts the dog and walks back two paces.

34. Finishing pose—Dog stands up on back legs and handler gives him a right-hand salute.

Starting and finishing poses

How you start and finish a routine is very important. A starting pose sets the stage for the routine and gives a hint to the audience as to what lies in store over the next few minutes. A finishing pose gives a definite signal to the audience that the routine is over and they can (hopefully) show their appreciation with rapturous applause.

SUPER STARTS

There are several different starting poses in the routines in this book. Two of the most popular starts with audiences are the salute and the dog in a basket.

The salute

A great way to start a routine is with the handler and dog facing each other or standing side by side in a salute (see Stars and Stripes, page 80)—this is a real crowd-pleaser. With a slight nod of your head, you can easily indicate that you are ready for the music to come in. The salute is a variation of the "face" command (see page 36).

Dog in basket

If your dog is small and cute, you could start your routine by sitting him in a basket (see Puppet on a String, page 89) or perhaps even a trash can (see Dinner for Two, page 113). To start with your dog in a basket, simply use the "sit, wait" command (see page 23). For the dog in a trash can, lead the dog over to the can and put a treat inside to encourage him to go in. Give the bow (see page 50), "wait" (see page 23), and "look" commands (see page 38).

FINISHING FLOURISHES

There are some spectacular finishing poses in the routines in this book. Two examples include the dog overpowering the handler, and the dog bowing from standing tall.

Dog overpowers handler

The "dog killing handler" move features in the Viva España! routine (see page 101). The handler lies "dead" on the ground and gives the "both" command so that the dog stands tall (see page 40). The handler then gives the "touch" command (see page 32) so that the dog drops

down onto the handler with both front paws. Be aware that some large breeds can be quite heavy! Lying with your arms crossed over your chest will offer you some protection.

Stand tall to bow

Another excellent finishing move is to have the dog standing tall and then dropping down into a bow. The handler can then bow toward the dog to signal the end of the routine. The Mack and Mabel (see page 119) routine uses this finishing move to great effect. You may need to use the "walk back" command (see page 58) to get the dog to walk away from you into position, and then the "both" command (see page 40) so that he stands on his back legs, followed by the "bow" command (see page 50) so that the dog drops into a bow.

STARTS AND FINISHES

- The salute (pages 80 and 82)
- Dog and handler standing together under twirling umbrella (page 83)
- Dog and handler shaking hands (page 86)
- Dog sitting in a basket (pages 89 and 91)
- A variation on the splits (page 94)
- Dog and handler doing a hand jive (page 95)
- Dog killing handler (page 103)
- Dog carrying a hat and going into beg position (page 107)
- Dog jumping over handler (page 110)
- Dog on back legs producing a bunch of flowers from handler's sleeve (page 118)
- Dog jumping over handler's outstretched arms (page 122)

A SIMPLE THREE-STEP SEQUENCE WITH PROP

To end a routine, nothing looks more professional than taking a bow. However, adding an imaginative twist with the use of a prop can really wow the audience. This three-step sequence makes use of a top hat, used as a prop throughout the routine. This can give a real flourish to the finale.

1 With the top hat on her head, the handler kneels down on one knee and bows to the audience.

2 As the handler bows her head toward the dog, she gives the "fetch" command (see page 31), and the dog gently takes the rim of the hat in his mouth and removes it from her head.

3 The handler gives the "leave" command (see page 30), and the dog drops the hat in front of him. He then sits, and the handler gives the "touch" or "tap" command (see page 32) so that he places one paw onto the hat. This brings tumultuous applause from the audience, while the handler bows next to the dog.

As a variation, or if the dog is very small, the handler may remove the hat to hold it out toward the dog as he takes his bow. The dog takes the hat, then step 3 of the sequence can be followed.

TRAINER'S TIPS

❧ Your dog needs to be completely comfortable with having objects in his mouth without chewing or playing "tug." This can take some time to learn, and it's best to train him using the same or an identical hat to the one you will use in the routines.

❧ Placing his paw on the hat is an extension of the "touch and tap" command (see page 32). Like humans, dogs favor either their right or left side, so to make it easier for your dog, give the command for him to put his favored paw on the hat.

Working with more than one dog

When I do demonstrations with several dogs, I am often asked how I manage to control them all. Because dogs are pack animals, there is always a strict hierarchy among them, and I take advantage of this natural pecking order to let them figure out their positions for the movements.

LET THE DOGS DECIDE

When I perform Mack and Mabel (see page 119), I work with two dogs on each side. During the practice sessions, the dogs were allowed to choose where they wanted to be.

All the dogs know where the heelwork position is (on my left side, with their head close to my knee), but although they all want to be there, they obviously can't. Kizzy, the most dominant dog, will never let another dog go next to my left leg. The next dominant dog of the four gets into what he considers the next best place. It would be pointless for me to try to dictate their positions, as the dogs would always be trying get to where they wanted to be.

ASSESSING A DOG'S ROLE

Different dogs will excel at different moves and paces. Choose which dog's paces best suit a particular section of music. For instance, for the Mack and Mabel routine, choose the fastest dog to work with the fast music, and when that music section finishes, chase the first dog out onto a circle and bring in a dog with a really good trot because the music will now suit this style.

If you are thinking of working with more than one dog in a routine, give careful consideration to the music and whether you can cope with all the dogs from the beginning or if it would be better to introduce a second dog later.

> ### PERFORMANCE NOTE
> 🐾 The Mack and Mabel routine is very fast in the beginning, and it would be difficult to control more than one dog. However, after the opening section finishes, the rhythm stays quite balanced and then it's an ideal time to bring in the other dogs.

Adding professional polish

Paying attention to small, important details that are easily overlooked will add a professional polish to your dance routine. Here are twelve top tips for you to follow to help you to win over your audience:

1 Watch competitions and demonstrations, in person or on video. Note which routines score well and which sections have the "wow" factor that audiences love.

2 Observe how well some handlers work with their dogs, timing their moves so that there is real synchronicity between them.

3 Do your research. For the Top Hat and Tails routine (see page 107), watch the film to see how Fred Astaire held and handled the cane.

4 Get a friend to help you to look after the dog as you change and to start the music when you are ready.

5 Acknowledge your audience with a smile, and take your time in setting up the opening move and signaling your helper to start the music. A slight nod of the head is usually sufficient—don't make a hand signal, as your dog might misinterpret it.

6 Ensure that your helper knows when to stop the music.

7 Have a video made of your performances to see what improvements you can make.

8 Get feedback from as many people as possible, even individuals with no knowledge of heelwork to music. Most of your audience won't know much about it either, but they will know if you and your dog look as if you are working together and if the routine is entertaining.

9 Try to add a little flamboyance and flair to your arm and hand movements. Stretch your fingers out to make strong, positive outlines.

10 Keep your head high, smile, put your shoulders back, and try to breathe normally.

11 Don't panic if you leave something out of the routine or your dog fluffs a move. Improvise by doing a few heelwork steps together until you can pick up the next section of music and start again.

12 At the end, smile, take a bow, and hug your dog. Just listen to that applause!

DANCE ROUTINES

Stars and stripes

This is a lovely, basic routine, and the beat of the marching music will really help you count your steps. Think of the arena as a square that you divide into smaller squares by marching down the middle and making sharp turns in each direction. Try to twist and turn your dog in rhythm to the beat. As you gain experience, build in extra elements, such as the dog reversing around you.

1 Begin by standing next to your dog. Put him in "sit" on your left side. Ask the dog to put a paw over his eyes by giving the "face" command. At the same time, give the audience a smart salute with your right hand. Now march forward for eight beats, with the dog creeping forward on your left side.

KEY MOVES: Sit, page 22; face, page 36; creep, page 46

2 Ask the dog to stand. You both turn sharp right, doing two clockwise circles together. March forward, give the command for two counterclockwise twists, then turn to face the front. Give the "down" command, then walk backward for eight beats with the dog creeping toward you.

KEY MOVES: In-place circle, page 42, twist, page 52; down, page 22; creep, page 46

3 March together in a fairly large circle for sixteen beats with the dog targeting your right hand. Change direction and repeat with the dog targeting your left hand.

KEY MOVE: Targeting the hand, page 26

4 March for sixteen beats down the middle of the arena, lifting your legs higher than before so that the dog can weave through them. Keep your hands down by your sides and stand in place. Lift one leg up and down in time to the music so the dog weaves through one leg for sixteen beats.

KEY MOVE: Leg weaving, page 44

5 Send your dog out on a large circle, where he canters around you in a clockwise direction as you skip in a smaller circle in the opposite direction. Ask the dog to join you in front and skip sideways, eight beats to the right and eight beats to the left.

KEY MOVES: Out on a circle, page 55; in front, page 24; sideways moves, page 34

MOVES

- SIT
- FACE
- CREEP
- IN-PLACE CIRCLE
- TWIST
- DOWN
- TARGETING THE HAND
- LEG WEAVING
- OUT ON A CIRCLE
- IN FRONT
- SIDEWAYS MOVES
- STANDING TALL

PERFORMANCE NOTES

🐾 I chose a classical marching CD featuring "The Stars and Stripes Forever" by John Philip Sousa, but you can choose any good march and fit these moves to it.

🐾 Remember to time how long the turns take when you are marching, or you will soon be out of time. This will vary depending on whether you are doing a 90°, 180°, or 360° turn.

🐾 Don't panic if you (or your dog) lose your place; simply march in place for a couple of beats until you can fit in the next move.

🐾 Although there are no props in this routine, you could adapt it, perhaps by having the dog carry a flag.

6 Repeat the hand targeting move, turning on each corner of a large square. About-face and march up the center line together. Next, do an in-place circle together.
KEY MOVES: Targeting the hand, page 26; in-place circle, page 42

7 Bring the dog into the "in front" position. Ask him to stand on his back legs, and give him a spirited right-hand salute.
KEY MOVES: In front, page 24; standing tall, page 40; face, page 36

Singing in the rain

Here's an excellent routine that utilizes a wide variety of moves. The whole routine is dependent on the umbrella as a prop. This is an ideal replacement for the target stick but can be an imposing object when open, so make sure your dog is comfortable with it before trying some of these moves.

1 Walk slowly but jauntily, with exaggerated steps. As you do so, the dog weaves in and out of your legs. Continue this for a number of paces while twirling the open umbrella.
KEY MOVE: Leg weaving, page 44

MOVES

- LEG WEAVING
- FIGURE EIGHTS (TARGETED MOVE)
- AROUND
- TWIST
- JUMPING
- BOW

2 Close up the umbrella and plant it down on the ground. Give the command so that the dog weaves a figure eight around you and the umbrella. As he does, keep swapping the umbrella from hand to hand, in rhythm to the music.
KEY MOVE: Figure eights (targeted move), page 65

3 Open the umbrella out and spin around counterclockwise in place as your dog circles around you in a clockwise direction.

KEY MOVE: Around, page 43

4 With the dog positioned on your right-hand side, place the tip of the open umbrella on the ground to the left of you and spin it clockwise. Now ask the dog to do counter-clockwise twists to create an impressive symmetry.

KEY MOVE: Twist, page 52

5 Kneel down and hold the closed umbrella out to your side. You will have to adjust the height of the umbrella according to your dog's jumping ability. Give the command for him to jump over the umbrella. Swap the umbrella to the other hand, and ask the dog to jump over it again.

KEY MOVE: Jumping, page 62

6 It's always nice to end with a bow. Put the dog in a heelwork position and hold the open umbrella over him. With your hat in your hand, lower yourself onto one knee and give the "bow" command to the dog. Hold the pose for the duration of the ecstatic applause!

KEY MOVE: Bow, page 50

PERFORMANCE NOTES

🐾 Rent MGM's 1952 classic film *Singin' in the Rain* and observe how Gene Kelly moves and uses the umbrella in such a carefree manner.

🐾 Use an umbrella that is long enough for the dog to jump over comfortably without it being too close to your body.

🐾 As a variation, open the routine with a simple walk to the center of the performance area, with your dog in the heelwork position, as you "whistle" the tune and idly twirl the umbrella.

🐾 The crescendo of the chorus, when Gene Kelly sings, "happy again," is perfect for the concentric circles or jumps (steps 3 and 5).

🐾 Add sparkle to your performance with some loose silver glitter from your pockets. Throw a handful up high in the air at the end so that it flutters down over you and the umbrella like twinkling drops of rain.

Match of the day

I first developed this sports-oriented routine for a British television show. The producers challenged me to train a complete beginner and a rescue dog to do heelwork to music in just four weeks. Even more difficult was the fact that they had to fool a panel of international experts into thinking they had been doing heelwork for years. It was very hard work, but they eventually succeeded!

1 Put the dog in a "sit" position. Blow your whistle, and with the soccer ball under your arm, jog up to him and ask him to give you a paw so that you can shake hands to get your "match" off to a fair and sporting start!

KEY MOVES: Sit, page 22; shake hands, page 33

MOVES

- SIT
- SHAKE HANDS
- DANCE WEAVING
- JUMPING THROUGH YOUR ARMS
- NOSE TARGETING
- UPRIGHT HIGH FIVE
- ROLLOVER

2 Still holding the ball, release your dog from the sit and dance from side to side with a 1-2-3-kick rhythm, transferring the ball from hand to hand as you go, while the dog dance weaves through your legs.

KEY MOVE: Dance weaving, page 45

3 Bend forward slightly and hold the ball out, positioning your arms so that they form a large circle. Ask your dog to jump through your arms. Repeat in both directions so that the audience has a good view of this.
KEY MOVE: Jumping through your arms, page 63

4 Place the ball on the ground, and ask the dog to start nosing the ball as if you are playing soccer. Pretend to chase him, and if you're feeling agile, attempt a couple of false tackles as you fail to get the ball away from the dog.
KEY MOVE: Nose targeting, page 27

5 Stand with your legs and arms quite wide apart. The dog is now going to try to score a goal! Encourage him to continue nudging the ball until he pushes it right through your legs.
KEY MOVE: Nose targeting, page 27

PERFORMANCE NOTES

🐾 This lively routine is ideal to perform for an audience that loves sports, such as at a youth club or school.

🐾 The costume for this routine is very easy to achieve—you can just wear a tracksuit and hang a whistle around your neck. A soccer ball and a lightweight children's goal will complete the picture.

🐾 Think of a theme tune or piece of music that is associated with soccer, and develop your routine around it.

🐾 Every move in this routine is counted for eight, making it very easy to learn.

6 Ask the dog to stand tall, and give each other a high five to celebrate.
KEY MOVE: Upright high five, page 41

7 Jog together in a circle, holding the ball under your arm. Finish the routine by lying down on the floor and rolling over together as you hold the ball in your hands. Do two rollovers in one direction and two in the other before lying still to signal the end of the routine.
KEY MOVE: Rollover, page 48

Puppet on a string

This routine has an exuberant feel to it. It was inspired by a famous 1960s song of the same name, sung by British pop star Sandie Shaw. It is ideal for a small dog who can act as a puppet, with you acting as puppeteer. You could choose any upbeat music for this routine, especially if the lyrics are about someone pulling at your heartstrings.

MOVES

- **JUMPING INTO A BASKET**
- **SIT**
- **WAIT**
- **FIGURE EIGHTS (TARGETED MOVE)**
- **STANDING TALL (TARGETED MOVE)**
- **IN-PLACE CIRCLE**
- **DOWN**
- **ROLLOVER**
- **REVERSING AROUND**
- **JUMPING INTO ARMS**
- **TOUCH AND TAP**

1 Begin by giving the "in it" and "sit, wait" commands so that the dog jumps into the basket and waits patiently for the music to start. Hold the prop out above the dog's head.
KEY MOVES: Jumping into a basket, page 62; sit, page 22; wait, page 23

2 Release the dog from the basket and, as he jumps out, walk around the basket together. Then ask him to do a series of figure eights around you and the basket, using the prop as a target.
KEY MOVE: Figure eights (targeted move), page 65

3 Time for the puppeteer to manipulate the puppet. Position the prop over the dog's head and ask him to stand tall. Now ask him to do four clockwise in-place circles.

KEY MOVES: Standing tall (targeted move), page 64; in-place circle, page 42

4 As the dog drops to his feet, give the "down" command and ask for a series of rollovers while you hold the prop over him. Now get him to stand and reverse in a circle around you.

KEY MOVES: Down, page 22; rollover, page 48; reversing around, page 61

5 Walk away from your dog, and holding your arms out wide, give the "up" command so that the dog runs and jumps into your arms. Give the dog a kiss.

KEY MOVE: Jumping into arms, page 63

6 Put the dog down in front of you and ask for a series of "touch and taps" to your feet in time to the music.
KEY MOVE: Touch and tap, page 32

7 Signal the end of the routine by sending the dog to the basket and asking him to jump in.
KEY MOVE: Jumping into a basket, page 62

PERFORMANCE NOTES

🐾 If you choose a song with lyrics, try to choreograph the moves so that they reflect the words in some way. For example, the line "I'm all tied up in you" from Sandie Shaw's "Puppet on a String" is an ideal point to fit in some leg weaving or a series of circles.

🐾 A small dog looks much more like a puppet than a larger dog and can fit more easily into a wicker basket!

🐾 You can make a prop from two pieces of wood glued into a cross. You could dangle strings from it if you wanted to. The other prop needed is a traditional wicker shopping basket, large enough for your dog to fit into.

🐾 Wear a nice bright top to reflect the happy, sunny mood that this routine evokes.

Cancan

It is said that the famous high-kicking cancan dancers of late nineteenth-century Paris were so talented and outrageous that they used to kick the hats from the heads of gentlemen spectators. Although this is not expected (or recommended) at a heelwork to music event, there's no doubt that the famous music will evoke an enthusiastic response from the audience.

1 Begin by standing astride the dog. With your hands on your hips, move forward together, doing a 1-2-3-kick as you do so.
KEY MOVES: Stand, page 23; between, page 42

2 Stand in the center of the arena and do a series of high cancan-style kicks. Ask the dog to leg weave each time you kick. Keep your hands on your hips as you kick.
KEY MOVE: Leg weaving, page 44

3 Standing still, cross your arms over each other in a Cossack-style pose. Lift one leg, bend it at the knee, and put your foot against the other leg. Now ask the dog to keyhole weave through the space. Repeat several times on both sides.

KEY MOVE: Keyhole leg weaving, page 45

MOVES

- STAND
- BETWEEN
- LEG WEAVING
- KEYHOLE LEG WEAVING
- CLOSE
- BOW
- CIRCLING AROUND

4 Bend over toward the dog, holding your skirt up at the back. The dog is in close and drops down into a bow.

KEY MOVES: Close, page 25; bow, page 50

PERFORMANCE NOTES

🐾 Try to find a dance teacher who can offer you some tips on how to do the steps and moves of this famous French dance.

🐾 Although the music of the cancan is fast, it is still a four-beat rhythm, and the steps are easy to count.

🐾 Thrift stores are a good place to look for costume pieces, such as a full circular skirt that you can cut down.

🐾 A pair of black fishnet tights, worn over the top of a plain red pair, looks authentic, and a pair of black three-quarter-length gloves completes the look.

5 Now stand on one leg, keeping one hand on your hip to steady yourself. Raise one arm in the air and hold one leg out in front. Ask the dog to circle around your lifted foot.
KEY MOVE: Circling around, page 54

6 Naturally, a cancan routine has to end with you doing the splits! Unless you are a trained gymnast, it's advisable to cheat, so just kneel on the floor, stretching one leg out behind. At the same time, ask your dog to drop into a bow. Throw both arms out over your head with an exuberant flourish to signal the end of the routine.
KEY MOVE: Bow, page 50

Saturday night fever

This routine is designed to bring out the disco diva in you and your dog! The stylish performance of John Travolta, who starred in the 1977 movie, was the inspiration. His charisma, plus his trademark white suit, huge collar, and platform shoes, suddenly made disco dancing cool. It wasn't long before club goers all over the world were trying to copy his moves.

1 Give the dog the "in front," "sit," and "wait" commands. Now lean forward slightly, and in time to the music, ask the dog to "touch and tap" your hands (or knees) so that you appear to be doing a hand jive together.
KEY MOVES: In front, page 24; sit, page 22; wait, page 23; touch and tap, page 32

MOVES

- IN FRONT
- SIT
- WAIT
- TOUCH AND TAP
- THROUGH
- CLOSE WHILE MOVING
- WALKING BACK TOGETHER
- DOWN
- CREEP
- TWIST
- STANDING TALL

2 Stand with one foot pointing forward, swaying in time to the music as the dog goes through and around. With the dog in close, walk forward together for four beats and back together for four beats. Repeat several times.
KEY MOVES: Through, page 42; close while moving, page 25; walking back together, page 60

3 Put the dog in the "down" position. Now ask the dog to creep forward as you walk at his side. As you walk, bend slightly forward and keep your knees slightly bent.
KEY MOVES: Down, page 22; creep, page 46

4 Time for a classic Travolta pose! Stand with one arm pointing up in the air and the other on your hip. Put the dog in front, and move your hand diagonally across your body in time to the music, twisting the dog clockwise each time your hand goes down.
KEY MOVE: Twist, page 52

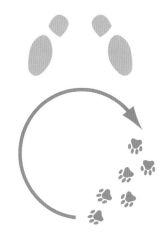

5 Stand still, legs apart. Give the command for the dog to run through your legs. Facing the same direction, give the "both" command so that the dog stands tall. Catch both of his paws with one hand and raise your other hand triumphantly in the air to signal the end of the routine.

KEY MOVES: Through, page 42; standing tall, page 40

PERFORMANCE NOTES

🐾 Watch some videos featuring disco dancing from the 1970s or 1980s. This will help you to find ideas for costumes and jewelry, as well as show you some of the moves that were popular.

🐾 Choose a well-known disco song that will help get the audience clapping and singing along as you perform.

🐾 Even when you are not moving, remember to sway in time to the beat of the music.

🐾 Stretch your fingers out, and keep your arms straight throughout the routine.

Calamity Jane

You're back in the Wild West, where horse-drawn wagons were the only means of transporting goods and mail from one state to another. There was plenty of whip cracking to get those horses moving faster and pistol shooting to clear the way as the wagons passed through hostile territory. This fun routine is reminiscent of those long-gone days.

1 Begin in the middle of the arena, with the dog in a "stand, wait" position. Stand over him, one leg on each side. Hold your arms in the air with the whip held horizontally. You and the dog turn in-place circles together.
KEY MOVES: Stand and wait, page 23; in-place circle, page 42

2 Hold the whip out in one hand and give the "jump" command so that the dog jumps over it. Repeat several times in both directions.
KEY MOVE: Jumping, page 62

3 The chorus of the song "Whip Crack Away" is an ideal point to hold the whip up in the air and twist the dog each time the words are replayed. Repeat in both directions.

KEY MOVE: Twist, page 52

MOVES

- STAND
- WAIT
- IN-PLACE CIRCLE
- JUMPING
- TWIST
- STANDING TALL
- TOUCH
- JUMPING THROUGH YOUR ARMS
- OUT ON A CIRCLE
- RETRIEVE

4 Stand, holding the whip horizontally behind you. With your back to the dog, give the "both" command so that the dog stands tall, and then give the "both" and "touch" commands so that he puts both paws on the whip. Walk jauntily together for a few paces, with the dog following behind.

KEY MOVES: Standing tall, page 40; touch, page 32

PERFORMANCE NOTes

🐾 Rent and watch some of those famous Western musicals from the 1950s for inspiration on costumes and music. The famous "Whip Crack Away" song in the 1953 film *Calamity Jane* is ideal for this routine.

🐾 This look is based on Doris Day's brilliant tomboy performance in *Calamity Jane*, but simple blue jeans, a checked shirt, and a cowboy hat will suffice.

🐾 You can buy whips of various lengths from most saddle shops, but make sure you secure the end of a whip properly so that it doesn't accidentally hit the dog or get tangled around your feet.

🐾 Alternatively, you could try making a mock whip from a long piece of painted cane with some dark twine attached to the end.

5 Kneel down on one leg and rest one hand on your knee. Give the "jump" command so that the dog jumps through the circle formed by your knee, elbow, and hand. The dog circles around you and repeats four times.
KEY MOVES: Jumping through your arms, page 63; out on a circle, page 55

6 Lie down on the floor, with one leg straight out and one leg bent. Hold the whip out vertically above you and ask the dog to jump over you, then throw your hat up into the air for him to fetch.
KEY MOVES: Jumping, page 62; retrieve, page 31

Viva España!

The end of this Spanish bullfighting routine is cunningly choreographed to ensure that the bull gets his revenge by killing the matador! The specially made red bullfighter's cape has a small lightweight dowel running through the top of it, making it easier to handle. It is a perfect prop for the dog to target.

MOVES

- STAND
- TOUCH
- BEG
- OUT ON A CIRCLE
- USING A TARGET PROP
- SCRAPE
- RECALL
- STANDING TALL (TARGETED MOVE)
- REVERSING AROUND
- IN FRONT
- WALK BACK
- BACK UP BETWEEN YOUR LEGS
- PLAYING DEAD
- UPRIGHT HIGH FIVE
- STANDING TALL
- TOUCH

1 Begin by positioning yourself in front of the dog, a few strides away. Hold the cape out and slightly down, to one side. Put the dog in "stand," and give the "touch" command so the dog lifts one paw. Drop down onto one knee and hold the cape up high.
KEY MOVES: Stand, page 23; touch, page 32

2 With the cape still held high, ask the dog to go into a beg.
KEY MOVE: Beg, page 38

3 Keep the cape high and straight up in the air while the dog circles around you.
KEY MOVES: Out on a circle, page 55; using a target prop, page 65

4 Stand, then drop the cape down in a swishing diagonal movement and give the "scrape" command so that the dog paws at the ground like a mad bull. Now ask the dog to charge at the cape, turning and repeating several times from each direction.
KEY MOVES: Scrape, page 32; recall, page 21

5 Give the "both" command so that the dog stands tall and reverses around you as you hold the cape in the air.
KEY MOVES: Standing tall (targeted move), page 64; reversing around, page 61

6 With the dog in the "in front" position, ask him to walk backward away from you, turn, and then back up between your legs.
KEY MOVES: In front, page 24; walk back, page 58; back up between your legs, page 59

7 Command the dog to drop to the ground and play dead. Hold your cape out and pretend to plunge it through the dog!
KEY MOVE: Playing dead, page 49

PERFORMANCE NOTES

🐾 Find a CD of some authentic Spanish matador's music to help build and maintain the drama of this routine.

🐾 Spanish matador music can be quite fast, but it is still counted in eights and dogs will find this tempo quite exciting.

🐾 Visit your local library to get ideas for a matador's costume. You can adapt an ordinary pair of black trousers by decorating them with gold braid, and embellish a plain jacket with shoulder pads and red tassels to give it a more traditional matador's look.

8 Time for revival! Walking away from the dog, ask him to run toward you and do a high five so that he appears to push you over from the front. Fall to the floor and ask the dog to stand tall by giving the "both" command.
KEY MOVES: Upright high five, page 41; standing tall, page 40

9 Give the "touch" command so that he drops down on to you, as if killing the matador. Repeat the "both" and "touch" command two or three times, then lie perfectly still as the audience applauds the dog's success!
KEY MOVES: Touch, page 32; standing tall, page 40

Mary Poppins

Fans of Mary Poppins, the fictional children's nanny, will love this magical routine. Not many people realize that Mary carried a dog in her carpetbag along with everything else! Our imaginary scenario begins with Mary giving her dog one of those spoonfuls of sugar she is famous for.

1 Begin by lying down and facing your dog, who is in a bow. If you like, you can get him to cover his face with one or both paws.
KEY MOVES: Bow, page 50; face, page 36

2 Time for that medicine! Ask the dog to sit up in a beg, and then pretend to give him several spoonfuls from the bottle with the spoon.
KEY MOVE: Beg, page 38

3 Place a basket on the floor and ask the dog to jump into it. Now drop to your knees and stretch your arms on either side. Tell the dog to jump out of the basket and over your outstretched arms in both directions.
KEY MOVES: Jumping into a basket, page 62; jumping over arm, page 63

4 Take your folded umbrella, plant it straight down on the ground, and cue the dog to do figure eights through your legs and around the umbrella.

KEY MOVE: Figure eights (targeted move), page 65

5 Sit down on the ground with your legs out in front. Put your arms out behind, and ask the dog to jump over your legs in both directions.

KEY MOVE: Jumping, page 62

MOVES

- BOW
- FACE
- BEG
- JUMPING INTO A BASKET
- JUMPING OVER ARM
- FIGURE EIGHTS (TARGETED MOVE)
- JUMPING
- WEAVING
- CIRCLING AROUND
- STANDING TALL
- TOUCH

PERFORMANCE NOTES

🐾 This routine was choreographed to fit to the words of "Spoonful of Sugar" (which, as everyone knows, helps the medicine go down). To help your research, rent and watch the 1964 film *Mary Poppins* starring Julie Andrews.

🐾 Be careful that the skirt or culottes you wear is not too long or wide, as flapping material can make it difficult for your dog to see the signals you are giving.

🐾 For the costume, you will need a red coat and a straw hat with flowers on it. Other props include a basket with a robin on it, an umbrella, a large bottle, and a wooden spoon.

🐾 This version of the routine, where the dog jumps in and out of a wicker basket, is most suitable for a small dog, but you can easily adapt it to suit a larger dog.

6 Kneel on all fours and give the command for the dog to weave through your arms as you crawl. Turn and sit down, then, in time to the music, lift your body up and down as the dog jumps over your knees, circles around, and runs under your back. Repeat two or three times.
KEY MOVES: Weaving, page 44; jumping, page 62; circling around, page 54

7 Ask your dog to stand tall and rest both front paws on your outstretched arm.
KEY MOVES: Standing tall, page 40; touch, page 32

8 Time to go home! Finish by opening up your umbrella, and as you hold it over your head, ask the dog to jump in the basket. Bend to pat the dog on the head, pick up the basket, and off you go!
KEY MOVE: Jumping into a basket, page 62

Top hat and tails

This routine was developed after I target-trained a dog for the first time. I wanted to do something involving a cane, and the wonderfully talented Fred Astaire was a natural choice for inspiration. I watched his videos, researched the music, and had my costume made. The tails of the suit are shorter than normal to prevent them from touching the dog. The top hat was a cheap one from a costume shop that I painted black.

1 You and your dog enter the arena with the dog carrying the top hat. The dog then goes into a beg, still holding the hat. Now you can take it from him and put it on your head.
KEY MOVES: Retrieve, page 31; beg, page 38; leave, page 30

MOVES

- RETRIEVE
- BEG
- LEAVE
- POLE DANCING
- JUMPING
- MARCHING TOGETHER
- STANDING TALL (TARGETED MOVE)
- WALKING TALL
- BOW

2 Put the top hat on and plant the cane down onto the ground. The dog circles the cane counterclockwise while the handler turns clockwise.
KEY MOVE: Pole dancing, page 56

3 Hold the cane out to the side and give the "over" command so that the dog jumps neatly over the cane. Repeat twice in both directions.
KEY MOVE: Jumping, page 62

4 Put the dog in the left heelwork position and give the "touch and tap" command so that he lifts his front paws and you can march together in place. Hold the cane up over your shoulder as you march.
KEY MOVE: Marching together, page 34

5 Hold the cane horizontally out in front of you at arm's length. Give the "both" command so that the dog stands tall. Walk toward the dog, who reverses away from you on his hind legs.

KEY MOVES: Standing tall (targeted move), page 64; walking tall, page 41

PERFORMANCE NOTES

🐾 Watch a film such as *Top Hat*, in which Fred Astaire dances with a cane. Observe how he uses it and the way he walks as he holds it across one shoulder.

🐾 When planting the cane onto the ground for the dog to circle around, make sure it is held straight and not at an angle.

🐾 Make sure the cane has a gold or silver tip so that it is easy for the dog to target.

6 Finish by planting your cane down at an angle toward the dog, removing your top hat, and putting the dog into a bow.

KEY MOVE: Bow, page 50

🐾 If you like, you can make a bow-tie collar for your dog to wear.

Let's rock and roll!

If you enjoy rock-and-roll music, you and your dog will have lots of fun with this routine. It's a high-energy, calorie-burning routine that will definitely improve your fitness levels. Although choreographed for a large dog, you can adapt it to suit a smaller one by crouching down as the dog jumps over you.

1 To begin, put the dog in a "stand, wait" position, then walk backward away from him for a couple of strides. Hold both your arms up in the air, keeping them wide apart. Release the dog, and as he comes toward you, bend so that he can jump right over you.
KEY MOVES: Stand, page 23; wait, page 23; jumping, page 62

2 Repeat in the other direction, keeping your arms clasped behind your back as the dog jumps over you from behind.
KEY MOVES: Stand, page 23; wait, page 23; jumping, page 62

MOVES

- STAND
- WAIT
- JUMPING
- CREEPING BACKWARD
- ROLLOVER
- SIDEWAYS MOVES
- WEAVING
- STANDING TALL
- TOUCH AND TAP
- WALKING TALL

3 Walk toward your dog, swaying in time to the music with your hands behind your back. Give the "creep back" command so that the dog goes down and back for four paces. On the fourth beat, give the rollover command. Finish the move with you and the dog crossing your feet simultaneously. Repeat the sequence.

KEY MOVES: Creeping backward, page 47; rollover, page 48; sideways moves, page 34

4 Kneel down and give the command for the dog to weave through your arms as you crawl. Position your arms carefully to make the move easier for him.

KEY MOVE: Weaving, page 44

PERFORMANCE NOTES

🐾 Ensure that your dog is physically fit enough to cope with this high-energy routine.

🐾 Leg weaving while you skip in time to the music is a lovely way of covering the entire arena and allowing the audience to fully see your dog.

🐾 Your costume should reflect your choice of music, and you could add that finishing touch by giving your dog a matching collar.

🐾 Listen carefully to the lyrics of your chosen song and fit the moves to it.

5 Ask the dog to stand tall by giving the "both" command, then give the "touch" and "tap" commands so that he puts both paws on you. Now turn in circles, repeating the "both," "touch," and "tap" commands so that it looks as though he's spinning you around.
KEY MOVES: Standing tall, page 40; touch and tap, page 32

6 Ask the dog to stand tall again and walk with you for four beats as you pretend to play air guitar. You can vary this by dropping to one knee and asking the dog to put both paws on your knee as you play.
KEY MOVES: Standing tall, page 40; walking tall, page 41

7 To finish the routine, sit down on the floor, hold your arms up and wide, and give the "both," "touch," and "tap" commands so that the dog is standing behind you with both paws on your left shoulder.
KEY MOVES: Standing tall, page 40; touch and tap, page 32

Dinner for two

This rags-to-riches-style routine provides you with a wonderful opportunity to dress up in your favorite ball gown. It perfectly suits a small crossbreed or one of those lovely terrier breeds that manage to pull at your heartstrings as soon as you see them. Our routine involves the Lady of the Manor finding a lovable rogue of a dog rummaging in her trash can . . .

1 To set up your opening move, walk with the dog in the heelwork position over to the trash can, which is placed on its side. As he goes inside, give the "bow" and "wait" commands. You can then give the "look" command so that he puts his head back over his shoulder to see where you are. Cute!
KEY MOVES: Bow, page 50; wait, page 23; look, page 38

MOVES

- BOW
- WAIT
- LOOK
- IN FRONT
- POP UP
- STANDING TALL
- TOUCH AND TAP
- CIRCLING AROUND
- BEG
- HIGH-STEP TROT
- RETRIEVE
- CLOSE WHILE MOVING

2 Now you can ask the dog to come out of the trash can. Put him in front and give the command for a series of "pop" jumps where all four of his feet are off the ground at the same time.
KEY MOVES: In front, page 24; pop up, page 63

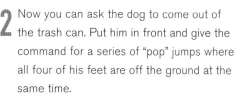

3 Kneel down on the floor and give the "both," "touch," and "tap" commands so that the dog stands and rests both front paws on your arm.
KEY MOVES: Standing tall, page 40; touch and tap, page 32

4 Remain kneeling on the floor as your dog circles around you closely several times in time to the music.
KEY MOVE: Circling around, page 54

5 The dog goes into a beg. He's trying to tell you something! This hungry pooch would love to be invited for a fancy dinner for two. Stand and walk together around the arena with the dog targeting your hand in a high-stepping trot.
KEY MOVES: Beg, page 38; high-step trot, page 65

6 Go over to the table, and as you kneel down, ask the dog to circle around you and under the table.
KEY MOVE: Circling around, page 54

7 Give the "both," "touch," and "tap" commands so that the dog stands tall and rests both front paws on the table. If you like, you could have some paper plates on the table and ask him to pick one up and bring it to you before returning to the other side of the table.
KEY MOVES: Standing tall, page 40; touch and tap, page 32; retrieve, page 31

8 With the dog in close, walk with him to the trash can. Put the can into the upright position, and gently lift the dog up and place him in. Give the "both" and "touch" commands so that he rests both front paws on the top. Kneel down beside him and support the can with your hands.
KEY MOVES: Close while moving, page 25; standing tall, page 40; touch, page 32

PERFORMANCE NOTES

🐾 Ensure that your dog is happy to go into a trash can. Placing treats inside will encourage him to explore. Secure a piece of wood to the front of the trash can to prevent it from rolling around when it is down on its side.

🐾 Create a bistro look by using a small table with a checkered tablecloth, complete with a wine bottle and unlit candle.

🐾 Clip the ends of the tablecloth to the sides or legs of the table to prevent it from slipping when your dog rests his paws on the table.

🐾 If you decide to wear a long ball gown for this routine, it will be awkward for the dog to do moves such as "through" and "between," or leg weaving, since your dress will be in his way. Use your imagination to choreograph some heelwork moves in between the prop work.

World of magic

The Internet is a great resource for magical props such as a "disappearing cane," but take time to practice tricks until you are competent and your dog is not worried by any of the props. This routine was choreographed for two different-sized dogs, but you can easily adapt it for a single dog.

1 Begin with the smaller dog standing tall and the larger dog in a "sit and beg." Hold your disappearing cane out, and put the larger dog into "down." The smaller dog then circles around you and jumps over the other dog. The next time, the larger dog stands so that the small dog can circle and run under him. Repeat several times.

KEY MOVES: Standing tall, page 40; sit, page 22; beg, page 38; down, page 22; jumping, page 62; circling around, page 54

MOVES

- STANDING TALL
- SIT
- BEG
- DOWN
- JUMPING
- CIRCLING AROUND
- BOW
- FIGURE EIGHTS (TARGETED MOVE)
- OUT ON A CIRCLE
- REVERSING AROUND
- USING A TARGET PROP
- RETRIEVE

2 Hold the disappearing cane out in front of you, and put the larger dog into a bow while the smaller dog does figure eights around both of you using the cane as a target prop.
KEY MOVES: Bow, page 50; figure eights (targeted move), page 65

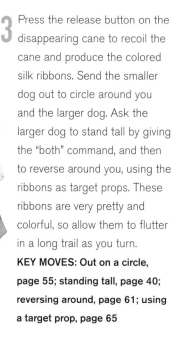

3 Press the release button on the disappearing cane to recoil the cane and produce the colored silk ribbons. Send the smaller dog out to circle around you and the larger dog. Ask the larger dog to stand tall by giving the "both" command, and then to reverse around you, using the ribbons as target props. These ribbons are very pretty and colorful, so allow them to flutter in a long trail as you turn.
KEY MOVES: Out on a circle, page 55; standing tall, page 40; reversing around, page 61; using a target prop, page 65

PERFORMANCE NOTES

🐾 Props for this routine include the following:

- A bunch of colorful disappearing flowers inside a cardboard tube, plus an elastic band to secure them safely up your sleeve.
- Disappearing cane filled with colored silk ribbons, both available from a magic shop.
- Silver dog collars to which you can attach some sparkling moon and stars charms, which will shimmer as the dogs move and add to the mystical effect.

🐾 For the music, there are many suitable classical compositions, or you may prefer to use a lively, comical piece and introduce some humor. Perhaps, then, if your magic tricks fail, the audience will think that it's all part of the performance!

4 As a grand finale to your magical routine, hold your arms out to the side and command the larger dog to come, stand tall, and retrieve the bunch of flowers from your sleeve (see page 30). As he holds the flowers in his mouth, both dogs circle around you. Finish with the larger dog in a beg and the smaller dog standing tall as you face the audience and give a flamboyant, low bow.

KEY MOVES: Standing tall, page 40; retrieve, page 31; circling around, page 54; beg, page 38

Mack and Mabel

This slapstick routine evokes memories of the bygone era of silent movies. The routine was inspired by the famous musical of the same name, which follows the career of Mack Sennett, king of the silent movies from 1911, and his enduring love for Mabel Normand, who went on to create the Keystone Kops. Four dogs are used in this routine (see page 76 for details on working with several dogs), but you can adapt it for one or two dogs.

1 Give the "in front" and "sit" commands to one dog. Stand with your right leg crossed in front of your left, and hide your face with your right hand. At the same time, give the "face" command to the dog so that he hides his face from you. Hold this position until the routine begins.

KEY MOVES: In front, page 24; sit, page 22; face, page 36

MOVES

- IN FRONT
- SIT
- FACE
- OUT ON A CIRCLE
- CLOSE WHILE MOVING
- HIGH-STEP TROT
- RETRIEVE
- STANDING TALL
- IN-PLACE CIRCLE
- JUMPING
- BOW

2 Now chase the dog out on a large circle, flapping your arms and mimicking an exaggerated Charlie Chaplin or Keystone Kop–style run as you go around the arena in an effort to try to "catch" him. The first dog leaves the arena.

KEY MOVE: Out on a circle, page 55

3 Bring the second dog in close, and move together around the arena as the dog targets your hand in a fabulous high-stepping trot.
KEY MOVES: Close while moving, page 25; high-step trot, page 65

4 Remove your cummerbund and ask the dog to hold one end of it. Turn and move slightly away from the dog so that the cummerbund unravels.
KEY MOVE: Retrieve, page 31

5 The dog now stands tall, and as he holds one end of the cummerbund in his mouth, you turn counterclockwise together.
KEY MOVES: Standing tall, page 40; in-place circle, page 42

6 Now hold the cummerbund so that it droops down into a loop at about knee height. Give the command so that your dog jumps over the loop you have formed. Turn to hold the loop out on the other side so that your dog can jump it from the other direction. Repeat.
KEY MOVE: Jumping, page 62

7 If you are working with more than one dog, bring the others in and put them on either side of you. Walk along as all the dogs target your hands in a high-stepping trot.
KEY MOVE: High-step trot, page 65

KEY MOVE: High-step trot, page 65

PERFORMANCE NOTES

🐾 The cummerbund used as a prop in this routine is made from the same lightweight material as the waistcoat. Secure it with a Velcro closure.

🐾 A compilation of music from the musical *Mack and Mabel* was used to choreograph this routine. It has a very fast section at the beginning, which is ideal for the opening sequences when one of the dogs is chased out on a large circle.

🐾 Watch some old silent movies and mimic the Charlie Chaplin–style movements to add comic effect.

8 Stand in front of the dogs and give the "both" signal so that they all stand tall. On a signal from you, drop all of the dogs into a bow. Don't forget to bow to the audience yourself!
KEY MOVES: Standing tall, page 40; bow, page 50

KEY MOVES: Standing tall, page 40; bow, page 50

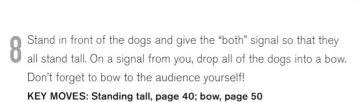

Into the swing

I have always loved swing music, and think I would have enjoyed going to all those wonderful dance halls in the 1940s, where people danced to live bands. This nostalgic routine is reminiscent of that era. I used a Glenn Miller compilation to give me inspiration and rented an American G.I. uniform to give it an authentic feel.

1 To begin, put the dog into a bow. Walk back four steps away from him, kneel down, and open both arms wide. Give the "jump" command so that he jumps over one of your outstretched arms. Remain kneeling until he turns and jumps back over your other outstretched arm.
KEY MOVES: Bow, page 50; jumping over arm, page 63

2 Put the dog in the "in front" position and dance sideways together in time to the music, twisting him on every fourth beat. Imagine you are jiving with someone, and exaggerate your hand movement as if you are literally spinning the dog around.
KEY MOVES: In front, page 24; twist, page 52

3 In time to the swing, with the dog at your left side, walk forward together for three and give the "touch" command as you kick together on the fourth beat. Now walk back for three beats, turn, and repeat in the opposite direction. Do this at all four points of an imaginary square.

KEY MOVES: Marching together, page 34; touch, page 32; walking back together, page 60

4 If you want to, bring a second dog in now. Keep one dog at the close, heel position and the other dog in front. You and the dog at heel walk forward eight paces as the dog in front walks back. Now you and the dog at heel walk back eight paces as the dog in front walks forward. Repeat.

KEY MOVES: Close while moving, page 25; marching together, page 34; walk back, page 58; walking back together, page 60

MOVES

- BOW
- JUMPING OVER ARM
- IN FRONT
- TWIST
- MARCHING TOGETHER
- TOUCH
- WALKING BACK TOGETHER
- CLOSE WHILE MOVING
- WALK BACK
- STANDING TALL (TARGETED MOVE)
- IN-PLACE CIRCLE
- PLAYING DEAD

PERFORMANCE NOTES

🐾 Listen to some jazz and swing music to get a feel for the rhythm and different tempos, then practice counting out the beat.

🐾 Swing is a carefree style of music and very easy to dance to. Don't be afraid to improvise and have fun.

🐾 Two dogs are used in this routine. The first is brought in for three minutes, and the second one is brought in for two minutes. It can be useful to do this in longer routines, as it helps to break up the routines and prevent repetition.

🐾 Glenn Miller tunes are so popular that audiences usually start clapping from the opening beats, so try to prepare your dogs for this noise in your practice sessions.

5 Hold your hands out in front, and ask both dogs to target your hands as you dance in a circle. Now ask them to stand tall in front of you and turn in a circle together.
KEY MOVES: Standing tall (targeted move), page 64; in-place circle, page 42

6 For the finale, drop down onto one knee, and at exactly the same time as you drop down, give the "play dead" command to both dogs so that they go down too. As the dogs lie with their legs in the air in front of you, bow your head and touch an imaginary cap.
KEY MOVE: Playing dead, page 49

Useful contacts

Australia
Canine Freestyle Moves Database
www.webforall.com.au/dogs/index.htm

Belgium
Dogs and Dance
www.dogsanddance.com

France
Obé rhythmée
www.obe-rythmee.com

Germany
Dog Dance
www.hundeallee.de/html/dog_dancing.html

Dogdancing
www.dogdancing.de

Japan
Dance! Dog! Dance!
www.caninefreestyle.jp

Japan Dog Academy
www.japan-dog-academy.com

Pawfect
www.pawfect.jp

The Netherlands
Canine Freestyle Nederland
members.chello.nl/a.wagenaar1

DTC Sport
www.dtcsport.nl

United Kingdom
Canine Freestyle GB
www.caninefreestylegb.com

Heelwork to Music
www.heelworktomusic.co.uk

Mary Ray
www.maryray.co.uk

Paws n Music Association
www.paws-n-music.co.uk

United States
Canine Freestyle Federation, Inc.
www.canine-freestyle.org

Canine Freestyle Magic of the Match
www.caninefreestylemagicmatch.com

Clicker Training
www.clickertraining.com

Dancing Dogs
www.dancingdogs.net

Musical Dog Sport Association
www.musicaldogsport.org

World Canine Freestyle Organization, Inc.
www.worldcaninefreestyle.org

Index

Acknowledgments

With grateful thanks to
Sue Evans, Sian Gearing, Kathryn Hardman, Avril James, Jan Morse, Lesley Neville, Gina Pink, Beryl Rounsley, and Carol Wallace.

Sports Connexion, Coventry CV8 3FL
02476 306 155

Ash, Bailey, Busy, Chester, Compo, Foxy, Ginny, Glen, Gypsy, Jazmine, Keya, Kizzy, Quincy, Robbie, Rooney, Saffy, Spice, Tazz, and Tilly

Executive Editor Trevor Davies
Editor Leanne Bryan
Executive Art Editor Geoff Fennell
Special Photography © Octopus Publishing Group Limited/Janeanne Gilchrist
Other Photography © Octopus Publishing Group Limited/Angus Murray/Steve Gorton
Senior Production Controller Martin Croshaw
Picture Librarian Sophie Delpech